✑ Table of Contents ✑

Foreword 5

Acknowledgments 7

Introduction: Buckle Your Seatbelt! 11

Chapter 1

Interest: The First Step to Reading Riches 21

Chapter 2

Background Knowledge:
The Second Step to Reading Riches 33

Chapter 3

Access: The Third Step to Reading Riches 45

Chapter 4

Commitment: The Fourth Step to Reading Riches 55

Chapter 5

Models: The Fifth Step to Reading Riches 71

Chapter 6

The Power of Discussion:
The Sixth Step to Reading Riches 79

Chapter 7

The Mystery of Gender Differences:
The Seventh Step to Reading Riches 91

Chapter 8

Technology: The Eighth Step to Reading Riches 103

Chapter 9

Rewards: The Ninth Step to Reading Riches 117

Chapter 10

Sense of Accomplishment:
The Tenth Step to Reading Riches 129

Chapter 11

Atmosphere: The Eleventh Step to Reading Riches 139

Chapter 12

The Brain: The Twelfth Step to Reading Riches 151

Chapter 13

Teamwork: The Thirteenth Step to Reading Riches 163

Chapter 14

The Secrets: The Final Steps to Reading Riches 175

Chapter 15

Your Challenge 187

Appendices

Appendix A: References Cited 192

Appendix A: Resources 203

THE READING MAKEOVER

Authors

Danny Brassell, Ph.D.
Mike McQueen, M.A.Ed.

SHELL EDUCATION

Publishing Credits

Corinne Burton, M.A.Ed., *Publisher*; Kimberly Stockton, M.S.Ed., *Vice President of Education*; Conni Medina, M.A.Ed., *Managing Editor*; Sara Johnson, M.S.Ed., *Content Director*; Joan Irwin, M.A.Ed., *Editor*; Kyleena Harper, *Assistant Editor*; Lee Aucoin, *Multimedia Designer*; Monique Dominguez, *Production Artist*.

Shell Education

5301 Oceanus Drive
Huntington Beach, CA 92649-1030
http://www.tcmpub.com/shell-education
ISBN 978-1-4258-1476-2
© 2016 Shell Educational Publishing, Inc.

৵ Foreword ৶

Charlie was one of my most memorable students from my early years of teaching. Blessed with a winning personality and plenty of charm, Charlie had been able to hide his reading problems throughout his primary years by cracking jokes, acting out, and mostly avoiding books. But by fourth grade with the increasing demands of reading both informational and literary texts, Charlie was clearly in trouble.

We all have at least one Charlie in our classrooms—and often more. Most statistics indicate that about a quarter of the students in any grade are reading below grade level. The bad news is that despite decades of research on reading instruction since I taught Charlie, we've made little progress in reducing the percentage of students who struggle with reading. And even more alarming, perhaps, is the number of students who can read, but choose not to.

That's where The Reading Makeover can help. Danny and Mike have put together a set of eminently practical and readable tips, tools, and techniques to "make over" the reading experience for reluctant readers. We've all seen the glitzy magazine makeovers where the drab and dreary candidate emerges with a new hairstyle, a new wardrobe, and a new outlook on life. That's just what Mike and Danny hope to do for reluctant readers; not with a new 'do and fancy duds, but through the power of teaching. Their aim is to transform dull, difficult, and downright deadly experiences with the printed word into celebrations of reading.

Early in the book the authors ask us, "What do you remember most from professional workshops you attend—the bulleted points on the screen, or the stories the presenter told?" In answer to their own question, Danny and Mike

have interspersed their own personal stories and anecdotes as readers and teachers into the research-based, professional advice. Between the covers of this book are many gems for reading riches, from atmosphere to technology, and attitude to teamwork. You'll read about hooking boy readers, tapping into multiple intelligences, and applying brain research. Most importantly, you'll see how your actions can help instil the joy of reading in your students. You will not only find The Reading Makeover an engaging read, you'll also gain plenty of ideas to make all students richer readers.

—Lori Jamison Rog

Author of *Struggling Readers:*
Why Band-Aids Don't Stick and Worksheets Don't Work

Education Director, High Interest Publishing (HIP Books)

‿ Acknowledgments ‿

A few years ago, I had the pleasure of speaking on the phone with Mike McQueen. He asked for my advice about public speaking, and I gladly obliged. Soon afterwards we met at a conference, and it was painfully obvious that we both shared a passion for making reading an enjoyable and lifelong habit for struggling and reluctant readers (who, let's face it, are predominantly boys turned off by the out-of-date classics too many schools try to force-feed them). I began formulating the concepts of this book when I presented my TED talk "The Reading Makeover" in December 2012, but this book would not have come to fruition without Mike McQueen. He is a good man and someone I truly cherish knowing.

Tim Rasinski introduced me to Teacher Created Materials/Shell Education over eight years ago, and I have had the pleasure of writing four books for them and consulting on numerous other publications. From its Founder, Rachelle Cracchiolo, to Rachelle's daughters Corrine Burton and Deanne Mendoza, the company has some of the most caring, innovative, and thoughtful leadership I have ever encountered in education. Teacher Created Materials/Shell Education have afforded me the opportunity to work with a talented team of editors and sales consultants, and I am grateful they have given me a platform to reach tens of thousands of teachers, administrators, and parents.

Finally (and most importantly), I want to express my sincere, profound gratitude to you. Watching the Academy Awards on television last year, I thought to myself how "badly" society needs another televised awards show for actors. Hey, I love movies as much as the next person, but let's face it: educators get very little respect. From janitors to bus drivers, cafeteria workers to aides, counselors to nurses, administrators to teachers...educators are too

often forgotten by society, particularly here in the United States. So this book is for you. If you are reading this book (especially the "Acknowledgments"), it is highly likely that you are an educator. You have one of the most important jobs in society: helping kids find their love for learning. You are humble and patient, loving and kind. You're amazing! Thank you so much for all you do, and I hope you enjoy this book.

—Danny Brassell

Acknowledgments

Writing this book with Danny has been an amazing experience and could not have happened without an incredible amount of support and encouragement from many people. Working on it while teaching full time, and also serving as a caring father/husband, has been one of the hardest things I've ever done.

Thank you to my loving family! To my wife, Jeanne, and my beautiful daughters, Makayla and Seriah. As you can imagine, I spent many late-night hours and long weekends with my face buried in my smartphone and laptop while writing this book. They have always been there to support my dreams and encourage me when I needed it. I'll forever appreciate their patience, strength, and love.

A big shout-out also goes to my mom, Carol McQueen, for her wonderfully spunky personality and remarkable ability to overcome so many hardships in life. Passing these great character traits on to me helped me get through the many challenges I faced while working on this book. Her cheerleading on Facebook did wonders, too.

Profound gratitude goes out to my close friend and author, Patrick Allen. Patrick was there for me multiple times throughout the writing of this book, giving me tons of support whenever I needed it (which was often). I'll always appreciate the deep, meaningful conversations we shared about education while hiking Colorado fourteeners together. Patrick has been a great mentor and someone I will always look up to—as a teacher, author, and Christian.

My perspective and experiences throughout this book derive from many amazing students, teachers, and administrators that I worked with throughout my career. A special thanks to administrators Deborah Gard, Judi Herm, Val

Braginetz, Sharon Ivie, and Cindy Stevenson. These five amazing women molded me into the educator I am today and each of them taught me how to be a caring professional. The teacher-librarian group from Jefferson County, Colorado also influenced me significantly throughout this book, especially Angie Wagner, Christy Yacano, Donna Ostwald, Andi Johnson, and Melissa Swenson. They grounded me in 21st century learning and helped me showcase the incredible influence we librarians have on struggling readers. They have profoundly influenced this book, which in turn, will hopefully influence you and your struggling readers.

Thank you also to my former student, Jake Hartman. Watching Jake overcome many challenges through his humorous personality and good heart continues to inspire me in many areas of my life.

Sara Johnson and Teacher Created Materials/Shell Education will forever have a special place in my heart. Thank you for finding me, for connecting me with Danny, and for believing in me as a writer. Thanks, too, to our editor, Joan Irwin, for polishing our writing and for keeping the project moving despite many obstacles.

Finally, I am incredibly thankful to Danny Brassell for having me co-author this book with him and for letting me share the reading makeovers I've been involved with throughout my career. Danny and I have so much in common— our own childhood reading struggles, our teaching experiences, our faith, our quirky sense of humor, and most importantly, our passion for students and teachers. Writing this book together took a lot of collaboration, communication, and teamwork between Danny and me, and I appreciate our journey together.

—Mike McQueen

⤜ Introduction: ⤛ Buckle Your Seatbelt!

Congratulations! If you are reading this sentence, you have proven you are extraordinary. You are a reader. Not only that, you are committed to reading and bringing the *joy* of reading to students.

Ah, there's that word: *joy*. When did exercises and drills become the accepted procedure in teaching students to read? How do those practices take the joy out of reading? Why was this allowed to happen? Do you agree with these changes? What good is teaching children *how* to read if they never *want* to read?

The Reading Makeover is designed as your personal guide to make reading a rich and rewarding experience for all those who struggle with reading or are so reluctant that they tend to avoid it like a telemarketer call.

In this book, we present a case for focusing on activities that engage students by motivating them to value reading and build confidence in their ability to read. This position is consistent with a large body of research on reading and motivation (Marinak and Gambrell 2008; Mohr 2006; Guthrie and Wigfield 2000).

Far too often, struggling readers are trapped in settings that inhibit—or even prohibit—their success. Well, the time has come to think differently and freshen things up for the sake of our struggling and reluctant readers.

Unlike many educational texts that are heavy on theory and light on practice, our objective in this book is to demonstrate for you how to ignite a passion for reading in your students. This passion is too often untapped in our schools. Our premise is that schools often become so consumed with meeting national assessment standards that they cannot see the forest for the trees. We ask you again: *What good is teaching students how to read if they never want to read?* We aim to help you create a different framework that empowers students with a love for reading. Each chapter of this book provides a different facet of this approach and describes steps for uncovering the riches that reading offers.

Brothers from Different Mothers

We, Danny Brassell and Mike McQueen, have shockingly similar backgrounds, personalities, and educational philosophies. Our skillsets complement each other. Because we are very excited to help both children and adults with reading issues, we truly are connected. Contrary to our similarities, our reading expertise derives from two different and unique paths.

Danny, the son of a librarian, grew up hating reading but has become a tenured reading professor and internationally acclaimed speaker on leadership development, motivation, and communication skills. He has taught all ages, from preschoolers to rocket scientists, and is passionate about providing energetic, informative, and highly interactive talks that inspire people to *read, lead, and succeed* (Brassell 2014). In his encounters and studies of leaders in education, business, government, the military, medicine, athletics, and the arts, Danny has seen time and again how not all readers are leaders, but all leaders are avid readers. He is dedicated to inspiring the next generation of leaders by enticing them with reading riches.

Mike also overcame his own reading struggles as a young boy and now receives international recognition for his expertise in helping struggling readers. He has spent more than 20 years teaching in a variety of at-risk schools. He served the first 11 years at the elementary level followed by nine more at an alternative high school, where he currently serves as a teacher-librarian for more than 800 struggling students each year. Mike has earned *highly effective* ratings throughout his entire career, and aside from writing books, he is also a keynote speaker and consultant with schools and libraries all over the world.

Together, we have created *The Reading Makeover* to combat the apathy toward reading that abounds in many schools throughout the country. Danny's work with leaders in a variety of fields brings him face to face with challenging situations that often call on his skills as a reader in battling student and employee fatigue. In fact, in recent years, Danny has turned to his skills in motivating reluctant readers to engage school and civic leaders by providing them with children's picture book recommendations that address teamwork, perseverance, communication, and decisiveness. Mike gets to see firsthand the day-to-day demands of teachers and administrators in trying to determine ways to meet educational standards without sacrificing student engagement. Recent implementation of new standards and increased standardized testing make it harder than ever to avoid getting lured into teaching to the test. Mike helps teachers stay positive by encouraging them, collaborating with them on different curricular units, and delivering professional development both formally and informally.

By drawing on our own common experiences as struggling and reluctant readers during childhood and our utter disgust as adults for the mundane activities too many schools offer students that drive them further away from reading, we are committed to making reading come alive for students so that they can experience its richness and become lifelong learners.

Our Classroom, Our Vision

As former struggling and reluctant readers ourselves, we know what it is like to feel embarrassed and discouraged about difficulties with reading. We understand how reading struggles can negatively affect one's self-esteem. Lack of reading confidence leads to reluctance, and this lack of practice results in what researchers deem "the Matthew Effect" (Stanovich 1986). Without getting too academic, the Matthew Effect means the rich get richer and the poor get poorer. So good readers tend to do more reading, and more reading leads to better reading in such measures as spelling, vocabulary, and comprehension. The opposite occurs for struggling and reluctant readers, who read less and find themselves falling further and further behind their peers. This situation becomes a vicious self-fulfilling prophecy where individuals who see themselves as poor readers literally become poor readers.

So, how do we make reading fun and desirable? How can we inspire our struggling readers and jumpstart our passionate readers when they go through a reading slump? We propose that reading instruction needs a makeover—one that will *inspire* teachers and *motivate* students. The landscape of reading has changed. Yes we think books are important, but so are magazines and newspapers. It is also important to note that we live in a digital world with a constant barrage of information in multiple formats. We need to teach our students how to gather, evaluate, and use information—especially with digital literacy. Like any healthy diet, our goal should be to provide balance and not overwhelm kids with "flavor of the week" reading programs. Although the emphasis on informational text in the Common Core State Standards (NGA and CCSSO 2010) has caused concern with some educators (Shanahan 2012/2013), we reiterate our point about the importance of balance. After all, is informational text any more important than literature or vice versa?

To paraphrase Henry Ford:

Whether you believe you can or cannot, you are right.

Our Purpose

Let's look at another important question, "Why is reading so important?" We all know reading is important, and we often say so to our students, but how often do we examine and discuss details about why reading is so important? At one point or another, most students will question *why* they are required to read something. Too often, adults simply say, "Because you have to," or "Because it's required as part of your assignment or grade in class." Without a good, inspiring reason to read, students will unlikely fully understand its relevance and importance.

We all have our own reasons for reading. We have witnessed how reading influences all areas of education and personal growth. Some say, "Good readers are good writers." Nonetheless, in our experiences as educators, we have observed that this is not always the case. However, neither of us has ever seen a good writer who is not also a good reader. The same can be said for leadership. Want to give kids a reason to read? Start with the leadership potential inside of all of them. Teachers can enable students to develop awareness of their learning and leadership potential through activities that sustain their reading motivation and expand their interests. These efforts are consistent with acquiring a "growth mindset"—the belief that one can develop motivation and productivity through dedication and hard work (Dweck 2007).

So how do we teach students to read? Learning to read is like learning to ride a bike. It becomes easier with experience, and we know that experience leads to confidence. Some would say, "That sounds simple enough." Remember this: people who say "that's easy" should be severely scolded. Anything is easy— once you know how to do it. The tricky part is getting to know how to do it.

So how do you teach someone how to read? The question of *how* one learns to read relates directly to the question of *why* one learns to read. We read to learn new things, and we read for pleasure, to be transported to different times and places and meet unfamiliar characters. Reading should not be about endless drills and recitations; it should be about stimulating discussions, solving problems, and thinking through different points of view.

Changing Practices

Contrary to what some may say, most people do not like change. They take comfort in knowing what to expect. Sigmund Freud called this "repetition compulsion," describing it as one's desire to return to an earlier state of things (DeName 2013). Schools, businesses, and people themselves become so accustomed to doing things one way that they are willing to ignore alternatives— even if the alternatives are more efficient!

Television is part of life. Computers are here to stay. The Internet is not going anywhere. People need to adapt to emerging technologies and embrace the advances they present, even as they relate to reading instruction and reading platforms. We are not advocating for people to rush out and donate all of their paperbacks to the next recycling drive; on the contrary, both of us prefer printed books. But getting students excited about reading is not about *our* interests; it is about *their* interests. (We will delve deeper into this topic in Chapter 1.)

The Reading Makeover offers practical and easy-to-implement ways to encourage students to read more. Some of the things we advise may make some educators wince, such as allowing children to lie on the floor when they read, encouraging students to be picky about what they read and discuss the merits of one genre over another, eliminating required reading lists, and scrapping desks in favor of comfortable furniture. Yes, we are going to "stir the pot" a bit and suggest some things that not everyone will feel comfortable implementing. After all, we know that every administrator, teacher, and parent is different. You have a right to make your own choices. If you need to hang on to the wall before you jump in the water, so be it. Keep in mind, though, what Christopher Columbus said: You can never cross the ocean until you have the courage to lose sight of the shore.

Change can be uncomfortable. Push-ups and sit-ups typically are not easy at first, but become easier over time. However, we know that the suggestions we make in this book have been proven to work in a variety of settings with a variety of students from a variety of backgrounds. You can use this book to help your struggling and reluctant readers. You might not be able to do *everything* that we suggest, but we urge you to do *something*.

What to Expect

We are grateful you are reading this book, and we are respectful of your time. You are reading this book because you expect to find solutions to your problems. If you are like us, you can get impatient flipping back over pages in search of specific quotes, anecdotes, or tips. Therefore, besides including some of our favorite quotes highlighted in quote boxes, we have also included chapter overviews, author testimonies, and reading makeover quick tips.

Chapter Overviews

When you were a student, did you ever have a teacher pause after each chapter he or she read aloud to ask the class what the main idea was? We hated that! We are not discounting the importance of understanding the main idea, but we would prefer to encourage readers to focus on enjoying the text rather than stressing about "test-question" points. So, to put your mind at ease, we have included brief overviews at the beginning of each chapter to highlight important points, the way journalists try to include the most important points in the lead paragraphs of their news stories. Now, if anyone inquires about the main idea of a particular chapter, you can quickly refer to the first paragraph of each chapter.

Author Testimonies

We have found that personal anecdotes are sometimes the best way to begin longer conversations about achieving change in teaching. In author testimonies we share personal stories and their relevance for your growth as a teacher. We encourage you to reflect upon your experiences and share them with your colleagues, and also with us by contacting us via social media. Let's create an ongoing dialogue!

Here is a snapshot of the type of information that you will find from our "Lessons Learned" throughout this book.

LESSONS LEARNED FROM MIKE & DANNY

Mike: I will never forget one of the most exciting and scariest moments in my life. My wife Jeanne and I had just gotten in the car, and before I started the engine, she said, "Wait, I need to talk to you about something very important." She put her hand on my shoulder, looked into my soul, and said something that was so deep, so heavy, so significant that I could not even comprehend what she said. I sat there in shock, paralyzed in disbelief, and the only words I was able to squeak out of my mouth were, "What did you just say?" She smiled, took a deep breath, and repeated herself.

"Mike, I think I'm pregnant."

Suddenly, my palms got sweaty, my hands began to shake, and I could not breathe. Three questions exploded in my mind:

1. What do I need to do?

2. How will things change?

3. How can I prepare?

After the shock wore off, I realized that I had my work cut out as a new dad and that my world was about to change. In education, we need to take a careful look at what we are doing and truly ask ourselves the same types of questions:

1. Are we doing what we need to for all students?

2. What changes do we need to make in our thinking, actions, and environment?

3. How can we change to better help students, especially our struggling readers?

Danny: A lot of people do not know this about me, but I am a weight loss expert. I have lost over a thousand pounds! The problem is that I have gained over 1,200 pounds, resulting in a net gain of over 200 pounds. My latest fad diet has been working tremendously, though. Would you like to know the details?

Well, for breakfast I'll typically eat half of a grapefruit, a slice of whole-wheat toast and eight ounces of skim milk (whole milk is deadly!). Then, for lunch I'll enjoy four ounces of lean chicken breast, a cup of steamed zucchini or broccoli and (to reward myself for doing so well so far) I like to enjoy a cookie. For my mid-afternoon snack, I usually devour the rest of the package of cookies, along with a quart of Rocky Road ice cream and a jar of hot fudge (sometimes I'll pour it on the ice cream, but more often than not I'll just drink it from the jar). Then for dinner, I typically eat two loaves of banana bread, and a large pepperoni pizza. For dessert, I have five Milky Way bars and an entire frozen cheesecake eaten directly from the freezer.

See, I have a bad habit—two, actually: I overeat, and I like to eat junk. Let me ask you this: Do you have a bad habit? I am so blessed to have a bad habit because it has taught me something important. It is much easier creating a good habit than eliminating a bad habit. I ask you: What good reading habits are we instilling in students? Do we use reading as a punishment or reward? Do we force students to read about what we are interested in, or do we allow them to follow their own desires? How are we instilling a value for the richness of reading in our students?

Reading Makeover Quick Tips

In this section of each chapter, we provide some ideas that you can use to help inspire others to read more. These tips are meant to be ways you can take immediate action without having to spend a lot of time and money. We want these to be useful and cause you to pause and reflect on some of the strategies you currently use. Again, we invite you to share your most successful tricks of the trade with us and your colleagues.

Reflection Questions

We conclude each chapter with a set of questions to help you reflect on the ideas in the chapter and how these relate to and affect your practice. Our hope is that these questions will prompt you to explore further, individually or with colleagues, ways in which you can support your students to become competent and confident readers.

Join Us on the Reading Makeover Journey

In the chapters that follow, we will lead you on a pathway to reading riches that will examine how to envelop struggling and reluctant readers with a reason to love reading and make it part of their daily routines. By the time you have read the stories, interviews, studies, and first-person accounts that solidify your understanding for best reading practices, you will have a better feel for how you can adopt these practices or adapt them to better meet the needs of your students. Let's make reading a remarkable journey for our students, remembering that a journey of a thousand miles begins with a single step.

So let's get on the pathway to reading riches.

—Danny and Mike

Chapter 1

Interest: The First Step to Reading Riches

In this chapter, we focus on why reading is important in the first place. We offer strategies that have worked in our own classrooms, as well as those of parents, teachers, and administrators who have participated in our trainings. The importance of choice is examined, as well as how to pick high-quality, high-interest reading materials for students.

If interest drives reading, it is critical that we facilitate an environment where students get to choose their own reading materials. As we take our first step on the path to reading riches, let's consider our role in creating reading environments that entice students to read.

All students deserve equitable access to an engaging and rigorous curriculum. To create classrooms that give students equal access to excellence, educators at all levels need to focus on seven interrelated principles.

1. Accept that human differences are not only normal but also desirable.

2. Develop a growth mindset.

3. Work to understand students' cultures, interests, needs, and perspectives.

4. Create a base of rigorous learning opportunities.

5. Understand that students come to the classroom with varied points of entry into a curriculum and move through it at different rates.

6. Create flexible classroom routines and procedures that attend to learner needs.

7. Be an analytical practitioner (Tomlinson and Javius 2012).

Here's a riddle we often ask people: What was your favorite textbook as a child? Please tell us if the word "textbook" caused you to pause. We do not mean to put down textbooks, but most of us learn the pleasures of reading by exploring novels, biographies, or nonfiction books and articles, not by analyzing random passages that cherry pick specific reading skills or provide historical or scientific information in a dry and mundane way. We have worked with seventh-grade boys who refused to go anywhere near a textbook, while those same boys would devour manuals on how to fix cars. Higher interest leads to deeper comprehension. After all, our interests usually build our background knowledge, and it is our prior knowledge that acts as the greatest factor in understanding what we read (Alexander and Jetton 2000). True reading occurs when we choose to do it for ourselves. For example, there are those who can spend months reading a textbook and not retain a word, while those same people can read an article about a subject they are interested in and retain information verbatim. Don't get us wrong. Textbooks have their uses, but they are not the typical resources that lead students to get excited about reading. We read what we want to read, so why not encourage students to pursue their interests?

Start with Why

No matter what type of reading material we hope to inspire students to read, our approach to the task is so important. Before introducing any reading material, lesson, or activity, it is essential for students to understand *why* they are about to do whatever is planned. By keeping lessons brief and making them relevant and meaningful to student interests, we will have a much better chance of getting students to be open. To paraphrase author Simon Sinek (2009): people don't buy *what* we do, they buy *why* we do it. This is certainly true for kids and reading. We must think differently and constantly justify why students must read whatever it is we want them to read. Student achievement requires motivation and willpower. In the long run, if we want our students to succeed, we must help them acquire focus and persistence in order to achieve long-term goals (Tough 2013).

Here is a thinking problem: You are sitting at a table. Ten flies are on the table. With one swat, you kill three flies. How many flies are left on the table?

We have received a variety of answers: 10, 3, 7, 0. What is the "correct" answer?

There are basically two types of responses that parents and educators supply students. One, they tell the student that he or she is wrong; or two, they ask the student for his or her thought process. We hope that by the time you are done reading this chapter you always ask, "Why did you say that?" or "Why did you think that?" The reason these questions are important is because, in our experience, students are usually correct. They may have a completely different rationale than the one we anticipate, but the more we seek to understand their thinking, the better we can meet their learning needs. *Their* why is no less important than *our* why.

Danny, for example, used to teach homeless Latino students at an inner-city preschool. Working with a four-year-old named Francisco, Danny wrote the boy's name and the word "Papá" on the whiteboard. When he asked the boy which word was which, the boy identified the word "Francisco" as saying "Papá." When Danny asked Francisco why he had pointed to that word, Francisco replied, "Because it's bigger." Francisco had associated the size of the word with the size of the person. That provided Danny with a better idea of why Francisco answered queries the way he did.

How many flies did you say were left on the table? A common answer is three. Remember, with one swat you killed three flies. The rest would have flown away immediately. However, we have seen plenty of students answer "zero." Do you tell them they're wrong? No. Ask students why they said that answer. On more than one occasion, we have had little boys argue that no flies remained since they swatted the flies so hard that the flies got stuck to the fly swatter. Ah—using that rationale, are those students correct? Always ask, "Why?" It is the essential question.

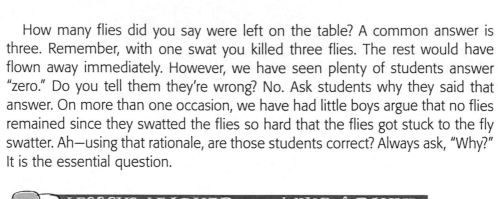

LESSONS LEARNED FROM MIKE & DANNY

Mike: It is human nature to share things that we like with our kids, especially great books that inspired us or changed our lives when we were young. The problem, however, is that often many adults go overboard with the concept and use pressure or guilt.

After a parent-teacher conference one night, a frustrated father marched his son into the library because his son needed to find a book to catch up on his reading "points" for class. I started talking to the boy to gather some background information, and within 60 seconds, his dad had already returned from the fiction section with a famous classic book in hand and said, "I read this when I was your age and loved it. Check it out, and let's go."

A look of disinterest came over his son, which frustrated the dad to the point of anger. I quickly stepped in, smiled, and diffused a potential explosion. I talked the dad into waiting just five minutes. After a few simple questions, I helped his son find a book he was really interested in and actually wanted to read.

The dad had good intentions, but his approach was disrespectful and counterproductive. The lesson is simple: If you force a book down a kid's throat, he'll probably throw up.

On a more practical note, I have seen many adults (including me) make this same mistake, but under different circumstances. For example, in my earlier years as a teacher-librarian, I would buy tons of nonfiction books on topics that I loved—hot rods, basketball, computers—and then I would always steer kids to them. Over time, I learned a better approach. Before buying anything for students, I would first try to really understand what topics they were interested in. Once the books were ready for checkout, I would still ask questions to learn the students' interests. I learned not to assume.

Modeling is one great technique I use to get kids excited about reading a particular selection. I model my interest in it first in a live "Book Review." I use body language (big eyes), inflection (excited tone in my voice) and various other forms of positive intensity (gestures). Imagine me standing in front of you, describing part of a book that I really liked. Similar to a movie trailer, I give you a one- or two-sentence summary about the book. Then, I share one specific part that I think you will find interesting: either by summarizing it or reading a super-short excerpt. When I finish, I raise the book up in the air, look you in the eye with a loving, caring smile, and joyfully shout, "Man! This book is awesome!"

Can you picture me pumping you up like this? Positive energy goes a long way. We will talk more about modeling in Chapter 6, but it's important to remember that if we want our struggling readers to be interested, we must be empathetic and show excitement toward reading. Otherwise, apathy often abounds.

Danny: People always ask me, "Why don't people read?" Well, essentially there are two reasons. First of all, there is a condition known as *illiteracy*, where people do not know how to read. Second, there is a condition known as *alliteracy*, where people choose not to read.

Both conditions are paralyzing, but I argue that there really is no such thing as illiteracy, only different degrees of literacy. For example, when you see a red light, what does that tell you? To stop, of course. We have over 300 DVDs in my house, but my own kids managed to figure out which one was *Finding Nemo* no matter where I tried to hide it. Children, long before they have ever set foot in a classroom, can identify McDonalds' "golden arches" from miles away.

Now, in my observations, *alliteracy* is the real "reading problem" we struggle with. We are becoming addicted to anything playing on the screens in our homes, at gas station pumps (video information screens), and in our pockets (the ironically named "smart" phones). It is alarming to note how many students opt out of reading in favor of games and other diversions on their electronic devices. Dinosaur curmudgeons like me cannot understand why kids don't read books, and we often fail to consider that today's students are growing up in a highly-interactive digital world that bears little resemblance to the one we grew up in years ago.

A fourth-grade teacher asked me to work with one of her struggling readers. In a little less than an hour with the young man, I observed him text friends on his phone, email nearly a dozen friends, update his status on social media, and research a variety of websites for items ranging from book summaries to nearby things to do for free. He was highly literate, but his teacher did not recognize his aptitude because it did not fall within her parameters for literacy. We will examine the role of electronic texts in the next chapter.

The research is quite clear: it does not matter *what* you read (Cullinan 2000). What matters most is *how much you read.* It does not matter if you are reading James Joyce or *James and the Giant Peach.* People who read more read better. I am on an airplane at least once a week, and I cannot remember the last time I saw somebody perusing Moliere, Dostoevsky, or Shakespeare, but I sit next to plenty of folks who read *People* magazine, *USA Today,* and trashy novels. Interest drives reading, so why not let students get behind the wheel?

The Power of Choice

One thing that all the superstar teachers, parents, and librarians we know have in common is that they respect their students' reading preferences. They give students plenty of time to free-read during the school day and ensure it happens at home. They make reading relevant to students' lives, they connect it with students' interests, and they do not let standardized tests pressure students into forced reading.

The concept is quite simple. Choice influences lifelong habits. On occasions when required reading is necessary to teach a skill or concept, students are more likely to buy-in if they feel like they have had ample time to free read books of their choosing. In fact, many experts believe that the majority of class time devoted to reading should actually emphasize self-selected reading rather than reading instruction (Applegate and Applegate 2010; Krashen 2004; Cullinan 2000).

Project-Based Learning

Project-based learning is a process where students take ownership in their learning by self-selecting topics (or sub-topics) that are interesting to them, understanding how to ask the right questions, and then finding the best answers through inquiry. Cris Tovani (2015) observes, "to promote deep learning, remember that students' questions matter most" (1). When planned and implemented properly, this approach can spark an intense desire to read, even among the most struggling students. Project-based learning promotes critical thinking, collaboration, innovation, teamwork, and technology.

As a teacher librarian, Mike has helped hundreds of teachers implement projects and has seen thousands of struggling readers come alive when they are allowed to learn about topics that they are passionate about. Finding, evaluating, and interpreting the best resources are paramount skills in project-based learning and can become a skillset that students use throughout their lives.

Visit Mike's website at www.ProfessionalDevelopmentForTeachers.com/Project-Based-Learning to learn more about this approach.

Reading Instruction Can Be Counter-Productive

Unknowingly, many teachers control too much of students' scarce reading time by over-teaching. Perhaps this is due to pressure from standardized tests, stressed out parents or administrators, or simply because of a good-hearted desire to improve their students' reading skills. No matter what the reason, we shouldn't monopolize valuable minutes during the school day with lengthy lessons, lots of lectures, or unnecessary activities. All these things can deprive students of the most important factor that will improve their reading attitude and ability—time to read materials that are interesting and meaningful to them!

In the following exchange, Mike discusses the importance of reading with Dr. Stephen Krashen, Professor Emeritus from the University of Southern California and author of *The Power of Reading: Insights from the Research* (2004).

Mike: Tell us about some of the recent research you've done.

SK: We looked at PIRLS (IEA 2011) data, and we analyzed what the predictors were… which factors predicted higher scores in general. We found that poverty, as usual, was the biggest predictor. High poverty means lower reading scores. We also found that the more free reading that a country allowed its kids, like sustained silent reading, the higher the scores. It had a modest effect. We found that if we look at the percentage of children in each country who didn't have access to a school library of over 500 books that nearly was as strong as the effect of poverty [very close]. That's why I think they balance each other. Then we looked at how much reading instruction affected reading. That was a low but negative predictor, where more reading instruction actually meant worse reading.

Mike: Wait! Are you kidding me? More reading instruction has a negative impact?

SK: Yeah, I think if you graph it out that you'll find from zero instruction to a little bit, it improves things. But after a while it has diminishing returns. People think [children] are bad readers so they need more instruction.

Mike: And why do you think that is, because they just shut down and they have a bad attitude?

SK: Yeah. Instruction is mostly mechanical and boring. Heavy phonics, for the most part...which is not what you need after a while. But a little is good, and after that the rules are too complicated. Phonics instruction, to make a long story short, helps you do better on tests where you pronounce words out loud. You don't need to know their meaning. It has practically no impact on reading comprehension tests, which has been confirmed again and again and largely ignored by people who make policy.

Mike: I have a really quick story to tell you that supports what you have just said, and it just baffles me.

SK: Yeah...please tell me.

Mike: When I taught sixth grade, I was a brand new teacher, and I didn't grow up as a typical teacher. So I was clueless about reading instruction and practice, you know—techniques and everything. And what I ended up doing in my first few years of teaching was mostly free reading and letting kids choose what they wanted to and showing and modeling excitement and modeling the journey and struggles that I went through. But really I just let them read independently.

The Progress in International Literacy Study (PIRLS), conducted by the International Association for the Evaluation of Education Achievement (IEA), is an ongoing assessment of reading comprehension at the fourth grade that has been conducted every five years since 2001. In 2011, 45 countries assessed nationally representative samples of fourth-grade students. The top performing countries in PIRLS 2011 were Hong Kong SAR, Russian Federation, Finland, and Singapore. Students with high performance can read, comprehend, and interpret relatively complex information in stories and articles of 800 to 1,000 words.

I let them sit anywhere in the classroom. I made it fun. And the biggest thing was that I didn't do small-group reading instruction. I didn't do so many of the things that nowadays we're supposed to, and I was so nervous the second year because we had to do standardized testing. The testing wasn't exactly what we do now, but it was the same concept.

THEN, at the end of the year when my students took the big test, I quickly looked and compared how much they had grown from previous years. I hadn't told anyone about my lack of guided instruction, and I was so scared to see how they did. I didn't think I taught as much as I should have. I let them read so much on their own. I read aloud to them every day, too. That was a big part of what we did for reading. But then I was like,

"Oh my gosh, here we go... how are they going to do?"

AND when I saw that they did so well, I mean...like about 90 percent of them showed such amazing growth, and I just couldn't understand how they did so well. I thought I was interpreting their results wrong, so I went and talked to the previous teachers. But sure enough, my students did in fact improve significantly. The outstanding growth my students made was kind of a mystery to me for years and years and years. But what you said supports that idea of not over-teaching and just giving them independence is a powerful tool in itself.

So there you have it—too much reading instruction is counter-productive. Wow, that seems controversial and may come as somewhat of a shock to some teachers, especially those who love standing in front of the class lecturing or rambling on. "Sit and get" is one of the least effective ways to learn, not to mention one of the most boring. Force-feeding information to struggling readers just makes their problems worse. As teachers we should be facilitators of learning, thinking partners, and advocates for self-directed learning.

Visit http://www.ProfessionalDevelopmentFor Teachers.com/stephen-krashen-interview-povertys-impact-on-literacy to listen to Mike's entire interview with Stephen Krashen.

The difficult challenge, however, is to determine how much reading instruction is considered "too much?" A lot of immeasurable factors come into play when trying to answer that tough question: age and reading level of each student, the amount of student engagement during the instruction, how interested each student is about the topic, and a myriad of other possible variables.

A good goal is to limit whole-group instruction to 10 minutes or less, limit small-group and individual instruction to three minutes or less, and then follow up the instruction with a variety of independent and collaborative activities. These suggested time constraints are not always easy to follow, but just remember that when students can control their learning, they develop a sense of ownership. This ownership is very empowering to struggling readers and can have a significant impact on their self-esteem and growth in reading performance.

Carefully plan your reading instruction so that your lessons are concise and transition quickly to independent activities that are fun, engaging, and also promote inquiry. During instruction keep a close eye on your timing and be cognizant of your struggling reader's attention span. As soon as you notice disengagement, be ready to adjust quickly.

Reading Makeover Quick Tips:
Connect Reading Materials to Students' Interests

- Get students to the library every week and make sure they know how to independently find topics that they are interested in. Ask a librarian for help.

- Talk with students often about their hobbies and interests.

- Stay updated about older students' interests by paying attention to what they post on social media sites or talk about with friends.

- Observe the types of videos students watch, music they listen to, and activities or games they like to play.

- Always let students reread books as many times as they want.

- Encourage parents to play "The Question Game" with their children. In this game, you simply take turns asking and answering questions on any topic that comes to mind.

Conclusion

The first step to reading riches is to create an environment that enables students to pursue their interests through self-selection of readily available, quality resources that represent a broad range of topics and levels of reading difficulty. In such an environment, students are encouraged to ask questions and explain why they think as they do. Choice is a powerful motivator.

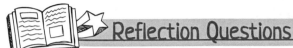

Reflection Questions

1. What are ways that adults can unintentionally be "pushy" with reading materials? Why is this a problem?

2. Textbooks have an important purpose in education, but how are they sometimes used in ways that can have a negative effect on our students' motivation to read?

3. Why is it important for students to self-select their own materials?

4. How can we encourage and motivate students to branch out and try new reading materials while at the same time respect their reading preferences?

Chapter 2

Background Knowledge: The Second Step to Reading Riches

In this chapter, we highlight Howard Gardner's (2011) research on Multiple Intelligences and examine different ways that they relate to the background knowledge of our students. We discuss ways to build background knowledge, share personal examples from our teaching experiences, and provide examples of how background knowledge has played an important role with our students.

The Importance of Background Knowledge

How important is background knowledge? Take this story about a woman applying for a teaching position in the Washington, DC public school system into consideration. In 2000 the Director of Human Resources, with the help from legal counsel dealing with Labor Management and Employee Relations, informed a woman by letter that she would not receive an offer of employment with the District of Columbia Public Schools, based on the results of the woman's criminal background check. The woman disputed the background check and provided the following documentation:

- her 1984 charge for Uniform Controlled Substance Act (possession with intent to distribute cocaine) was no papered

- her 1984 charge for shoplifting was nolle prosequi

- her 1984 charge for assault with a dangerous weapon (a razor) was no papered

- her 1984 charge for destruction of government property was nolle prosequi

- her 1986 charge for assault with a deadly weapon was dismissed

- her 1987 charge for soliciting for prostitution was nolle prosequi

- her 1989 charge for assault with a dangerous weapon (razor) was no papered

- her 1992 charge for Uniform Controlled Substance Act was dismissed

No papered means that a person arrested for a crime was never charged, and the prosecutor has declined to file charges and prosecute.

Nolle prosequi means the prosecutor initially sought indictment but opted not to proceed before the grand jury returned its findings.

After receiving the woman's subsequent presentation of documentation, the Human Resources Department determined that the woman was eligible for employment to teach, since she was never actually convicted of anything (Barras 2001).

Does a little background knowledge affect your opinion of this woman if she was teaching your child? How important do think it would be for you to know such information? Now, think of the students in your classroom. Do you see any value in learning something about *their* backgrounds?

Discovering How Students Learn

Background knowledge matters. As teachers, we want our students to learn how to tap into their prior knowledge, how to use it effectively, and—most importantly—how to build on it, so they can be critical, independent readers and thinkers. No matter the topic, we cannot make any assumptions about students' prior knowledge. Assessing *what* students know is critical; but first, teachers must discover *how* students learn.

Considering Classroom Environment

It is important to understand how students learn best. The physical environment plays a vital role. For example, noise level matters. Does the student work better in a noisy or quiet environment? We love students who are enthusiastic about reading and eager to share interesting pictures or passages to classmates, but we are also aware that these students may be distracting to others and need to sit in a different part of the classroom. Besides noise level, the physical arrangement of the room plays a crucial role in maximizing student learning. Does the room arrangement support too much structure, or does it promote independent and flexible learning? Some students know exactly what they want to read, while others may browse shelves for infinite amounts of time without guidance from a teacher to show them how to choose something to read. Does the student work better alone or with others? Does the room arrangement support this? Our experience with English language learners shows that "partnering" students during reading times can greatly improve their reading aptitudes and attitudes.

Understanding Motivation Factors

This brings us to perhaps the most important thing for teachers to consider—a student's motivation level. Does the student typically move from task to task rapidly, or engage in a single activity for an extended period of time? Just because a student decides to change reading materials from time to time does not mean that student is not an interested or talented reader. On the contrary, "picky" readers, in our experiences, often tend to be better readers. We live in a digital age where students are bombarded with information. They need to learn how to quickly discriminate useful information from that which is not as important or that which does not interest them. Does every student absolutely have to read *A Separate Peace* (Knowles 2003), or should there be some leeway in allowing students to select books related to topics that intrigue them? Maybe a student reading John Knowles for the first time suddenly feels the urge to learn more about prep schools in New England. Should we prevent that student from further investigation? Put another way, are you more motivated to do things you are *told* to do, or activities you get to *select* yourself? If we are striving to inspire students to read more (and, as a result, become better readers), we are certain to have greater success by allowing students to follow their own curiosity and letting them know that being picky about reading choices is okay.

Understanding Emotional Intelligence

It is also helpful for teachers to understand a student's emotional intelligence—the ability to use his or her emotions intelligently and maintain a balance between reason and emotion (Goleman 2005). Teachers should observe student behaviors and ask themselves a variety of questions.

- **How much self-awareness does the child possess?** We like to often facilitate a "Think-Pair-Share" approach to our read-alouds where students reflect on how a reading passage relates to their own experiences, discuss their experiences with a partner, and then share their experiences with the entire class. Using this approach is helpful in determining if students have the ability to name a feeling when it happens and how we can recognize and manage their moods.

- **What problem-solving skills does the student possess?** We like to constantly pose challenging scenario questions to students to determine how they would address different situations. For example, when Danny was a history teacher, he reminded students that history books are usually "written by the winners" (in battles, scenarios, and struggles), and he challenged students to consider problems from multiple points of view.

- **How persistent is the student? Does he or she give up easily or see things through?** One of the reasons we love to encourage students to read in our classes is because it tells us a lot about student interest, attention levels, and ability to stay on task.

- **What sort of empathy does the student show for others, and does he or she comprehend situations and cues?** Reading with a student is a great way to assess his or her emotional intelligence. One of the reasons we love reading aloud to our classes is because it provides students a forum to question how they and others view similar events in various or identical ways.

Understanding Multiple Intelligences

It is critical to determine what Harvard professor Howard Gardner (2011) deems students' "multiple intelligences." Gardner suggests that while students may all be expected to learn the same content, they have different ways of learning that content. Gardner asserts that students exhibit their knowledge in eight different ways, as shown in Figure 2.1 (Nicholson-Nelson 1998). Each student is an individual learner with a different preferred learning style. Is the student an auditory learner who favors listening to lectures, stories, and songs? Perhaps the student is a tactile learner who enjoys concrete experiences like handling materials, writing, and drawing. Does the student prefer the physical activity of a kinesthetic learner who likes doing and moving? Or, is the student a visual learner who benefits from colors and graphic organizers as well as illustrations, pictures, and diagrams?

Figure 2.1 Eight Multiple Intelligences

Gardner's Intelligence Area	Strengths	Enjoys	Preferred Learning Strategies
Verbal-Linguistic	reading, writing, telling stories, memorizing dates, thinking in words	reading, writing, telling stories, talking, memorizing, working at puzzles	reading, hearing and seeing words, speaking, writing, discussing and debating
Logical-Mathematic	math, reasoning, logic, problem solving, patterns	solving problems, questioning, working with numbers, experimenting	working with patterns and relationships, classifying, categorizing, working with the abstract
Spatial	reading, maps, charts, drawing, mazes, puzzles, imagining things, visualizing	designing, drawing, building, creating, daydreaming, looking at pictures	working with pictures and colors, visualizing, using the mind's eye, drawing
Bodily-Kinesthetic	athletics, dancing, acting, crafting, using tools	moving around, touching, talking, body language	touching, moving, processing knowledge through bodily sensations
Musical	singing, picking up sounds, remembering melodies, rhythms	singing, humming, playing an instrument, listening to music	rhythm, melody, singing, listening to music and melodies

Gardner's Intelligence Area	Strengths	Enjoys	Preferred Learning Strategies
Interpersonal	understanding people, leading, organizing, communicating, resolving conflicts, selling	having friends, talking to people, joining groups	sharing, comparing, relating, interviewing, cooperating
Intrapersonal	understanding self, recognizing strengths and weaknesses, setting goals	working alone, reflecting, pursuing interests	working alone, doing self-paced projects, needing space, reflecting
Naturalist	understanding nature, making distinctions, identifying flora and fauna	being involved with nature, making distinctions	working in nature, exploring living things, learning about plants and natural events

Adapted from Gardner (2011)

Assessing Students' Reading Abilities and Interests

To determine which way of *being smart* children prefer, teachers can engage in meaningful dialogues with students by asking them lots of questions and listening to the answers provided. By keeping pre-assessments simple and fun (through observation checklists, inventories, logs, journals, graphic organizers, and a variety of other informal and formal assessment procedures), teachers can determine *how* students like to learn and adapt their reading instruction accordingly. For example, reading observation checklists can be used to hone in on whether a student usually, sometimes, or hardly ever (we simply note behaviors with "+, √, or −" signs) exhibits behaviors such as frequently talking about books he or she likes/dislikes, identifying high-frequency words, and reading with expression. Additionally, reading inventory checklists that identify a student's favorite reading genre(s), how often he or she reads at home, and how much a student enjoys reading can provide critical information in how we approach building that student's reading interest and skills. Graphic organizers like Venn diagrams, K-W-L + charts, and semantic maps are helpful in determining a wide range of things about students—from what they like to read to their reading comprehension and reasoning skills. The point is, assessments do not have to be drab or highly formal in order to provide teachers with an abundance of useful information in helping students read better and more frequently.

Building Students' Background Knowledge

Gina Cervetti and Elfrieda Hiebert (2015) maintain that knowledge development is an essential component of effective literacy instruction. Consequently, teachers need to understand what students know in order to help them grow in their understanding of new ideas and concepts. The only background knowledge we can be certain of is that which we create with students in our classrooms. Students may come to class with vastly different experiences, but teachers can enhance students' background knowledge in a variety of ways. They may model for students how to locate books of interest or where to locate information. They may use souvenirs—showing students a prompt and asking them questions or providing stories related to the prompt. For example, if you were about to conduct a unit on dinosaurs, you could show students a fossil and ask them where they thought it originated. Since we have taught a number of English language learners, we have also found it useful to preview lessons with specific vocabulary words to get a better sense of what students know. Additionally, it may sound old-fashioned, but we insist that Show and Tell is a critical strategy in gaining a better understanding of students' background knowledge. We often encourage students to bring art, music, and other items from home that help us learn more about their backgrounds and interests.

It is important for teachers to accurately assess students' background knowledge on various subjects. It is equally important to avoid assuming students lack background knowledge. This misconception can be offensive to a student and lead to disengagement and distrust. Although some students may come across as knowing it all, you may find it useful to prompt them to explain themselves to determine the extent and depth of their background knowledge. For example, invite students to tell more or explain where they learned about or discovered the information. Most students know a lot of information about a variety of different topics, and the same is true for struggling readers. They may be battling some type of reading challenge, but they will often build their background knowledge through other methods, such as watching television, talking with friends and relatives, and surfing the Internet. Teachers can avoid embarrassment by asking lots of questions and paying close attention to

Tips for Morning Meetings

Danny used to have his students run morning meetings like a news broadcast. He modeled it for a couple of weeks, did it with the students for a couple of weeks, and then handed the reins to the students to run the show. Morning meetings typically last 30—45 minutes and are useful ways to address a range of learning and curricular topics. In his classroom, morning meetings followed this format:

- **Circle of Life:** students sing and chant

- **Daily News:** a student "anchor person" reads aloud which students are to lead the different activities during the day's morning meeting

- **Weather:** a student "meteorologist" reads aloud the day's weather forecast, following a pre-set format (for example, "The temperature today will be __," and so on)

- **Famous Birthdays:** a student reads aloud a short passage listing some famous birthdays for the day, including a brief biography of one specific famous person

- **Thought of the Day:** a student reads aloud an inspirational quote or short piece of poetry and leads a class discussion on what the "thought of the day" means to the class

- **Personal Profile:** also known as "show and tell," where one student shares personal information with the class

- **Day's Agenda:** a student reads aloud the activities the class will be doing for the day

- **Class Goals and Objectives:** a student reads aloud the standards that will be covered during the day

students' interests. One of the reasons we encourage students to run a daily Morning Meeting (Kriete and Davis 2014) is to allow them to use their own experiences to talk about what they have read or learned.

Reading Makeover Quick Tips: Build on Background Knowledge

- Encourage student-led literacy activities throughout the day (for example, Morning Meetings).

- During transition times, ask students questions to determine what they know. You can even turn it into a game (e.g., ask students to take the number of original U.S. colonies, add it to the number of characters in a book they just read, and then subtract the number of planets in our galaxy).

- Provide a wide range of reading materials at different degrees of difficulty so all students have the opportunity to read about a topic at their level.

- Use timely newspaper and Internet articles to facilitate classroom discussions.

- Take field trips. If your school does not get many field trips, bring the world to your classroom by inviting guest speakers (e.g., international students, business people, community leaders, and so on).

- Take virtual field trips via the Internet (e.g., tour the Capitol or visit the Metropolitan Museum of Art's website).

- When you read aloud to students, think aloud (meaning: verbally describe to students the questions and thoughts that pop into your mind as you read).

- Encourage students to watch documentaries, listen to speeches, and attend presentations in their communities and at their local libraries.

LESSONS LEARNED FROM MIKE & DANNY

Mike: In the second year of our elementary school's reading makeover, Teacher of the Year Sharon Ivie came to our school as our instructional coach. I remember how great she was with modeling to both students and staff various reading and writing activities. She taught me the correct process of project-based learning and how to look for ways to make connections with what students already knew. Sharon was magical in getting students to share their prior knowledge, to ask lots of questions, and to develop a hunger to learn more.

After working with Sharon, I went on to collaborate with many other teachers on a wide range of curricular units. No matter what topic a class was about to study, at the beginning of every unit, we engaged in some type of activity that explained what we were about to study and why it was important to learn.

Kimberly Willahan is an amazing English teacher with whom I have worked for many years. I asked Kimberly to suggest one effective technique that builds background knowledge with her students, and she reminded me of many different projects that I have helped her with that involve using images and visual information to spark an interest that will lead to more reading. She suggests to have students build their background knowledge by researching with Google Earth. Google Earth is a free online program that allows students to locate anything on Earth through satellite imaging. Not only is Google Earth fun, cool, and extremely interactive, it inspires students to do more research.

Danny: On my first day of teaching elementary school, I was completely lost. Random bells would ring throughout the day, and I had no idea whether they meant that it was time for recess or if the school was on fire. Besides not knowing the bell schedule, I did not know there was a faculty restroom among other things. Basically, I was left to fend for myself.

At first, teaching felt like when I studied in Spain. It was an entirely new culture that I had to learn. So when I stared into the eyes of struggling and reluctant readers (mostly boys), I could empathize with their frustrations.

Getting to know your students is like learning a new culture. It may take time, but it is critical to learn as much about them as you can. The more I understand what my students know and how they learn new information, the better equipped I am to maximize their learning. While I used poetry and songs to inspire most of my students, there were some who preferred sitting on their own and enjoying their own activities. What I have learned over the years is that schools are supposed to be about kids, not teachers. We need to be the ones to adapt, not the students.

Carl Jung (1939) once said, "If there is something we wish to change in the child, we should first examine it and see whether it is not something that could be better changed in ourselves" (285).

I have learned that it is better to let students take the lead initially to see where they take me. When they signal an interest in nonfiction, we tackle nonfiction. If they prefer comprehension activities that encourage them to act-out stories, that is what we do. Making assumptions is the death of any teacher. The more we get to know what students know and how they like to learn, the better we can serve them.

Conclusion

Background knowledge plays an important role in reading. Knowing the intelligence area(s) of your readers, especially those who struggle, can help determine the best approach to maximize their success. Before starting a new book or instructional unit, provide activities that allow students to access and share their prior experiences. Every struggling reader has skills and strengths that can be paired with reading. We encourage you to consider that you can learn a lot about how students learn and what they already know through inspiring and engaging activities. It is your job to help them find their talents and make connections to new ideas.

 Reflection Questions

1. In what ways do you access your background knowledge in your personal and/or professional life?

2. Looking at Gardner's Eight Multiple Intelligences, in which areas are you strong? Think about one of your students who struggles with reading. In which areas is that student strong?

3. Why is it important to access background knowledge when learning something new?

4. What are different ways to connect background knowledge with different types of reading materials, such as magazines, fiction and nonfiction books, digital resources, or comics?

44

Access: The Third Step to Reading Riches

To help students become successful readers, it is vital to provide them with enough reading materials that match their interests. In this chapter we explain the importance of reading immersion and provide a wide range of ideas and techniques that will help build your classroom's reading collection.

Resources Matter

A famous film director appeared on a national talk show. When the show's host asked the director about his views on parenting, the director confessed that his seven children presented plenty of challenges, as well as opportunities. When asked to elaborate, he shared that he viewed his primary role, as a father, was to provide his children with opportunities to succeed. The director revealed that every room of his family's home had a video camera, so whenever his children felt the urge to film, they had instant access to a video camera. What do you think the odds are that one of his children pursued a career in the entertainment industry?

Have you ever wondered why there are not many professional surfers from Nebraska or ice skaters from Kenya? Would you be surprised to learn that people without credit cards tend to spend less than those with credit cards? Resources matter. Stephen Krashen (2005) reports that the amount of reading

one does is directly correlated to the reading environment that surrounds them. In other words, the more reading resources and materials that exist within a home or classroom, the more reading its inhabitants will do. That means we must get to work building literacy-rich environments for our students because access matters.

Reading Immersion

As caring adults, we want reading to be a part of our students' everyday lives. We want students to be so excited about reading that when they talk about books, magazines, authors, or anything else reading related, their faces light up with anticipation. We want our students surrounded, immersed in attractive and engaging reading opportunities, activities, discussions, and materials. These materials need to be accessible everywhere—at home, at school, in sports facilities, in vehicles, on vacation, and any other possible opportunities.

The key components to reading immersion are: enough access to quality reading materials and the correct guidance that inspires students to obtain and read the materials. Stephen Krashen (2013) found that access leads to free voluntary reading, as well. Having access to enough quality reading materials is critically important. There is always a logical explanation that prevents students from having access to the quality and quantity of reading materials they need. Perhaps the student lives in a single-parent household where the parent has three jobs and cannot secure books or does not understand the importance of reading when basic needs are barely being met. Maybe the student is going through a family crisis, or maybe the family just relies on the school system because they feel inadequate or incapable of helping. Perhaps it is the expectation in their culture that reading happens at school. Overwhelmingly, the research suggests that students from impoverished households are at a significant disadvantage to their peers when it comes to access to books (Krashen 2005; Neuman and Celano 2001). Not only do they have fewer books in their homes, these students live in communities that have less access to books in their classrooms, schools, and even public libraries.

If we truly want to have a successful *reading makeover*, we need to get to the bottom of any possible barriers by thoroughly investigating each situation, clearly defining the problem, recruiting help if needed, making a plan to improve the situation, and following through to make changes and improvements. Learning about possible barriers may mean holding parent workshops, conducting a book drive, hosting evening or weekend events, re-decorating the environment, visiting a student's home, or simply reminding students and parents to make reading part of their daily routine.

Getting Reading Materials

Both of us have a lot of experience in securing reading materials for our students. There are a number of sources to support with this endeavor, and they are not always obvious.

Be sure to take advantage of your local library where thousands of titles are available to be checked out for weeks at a time. Ideally, every student, *especially* struggling readers, should visit the library at least once a week from birth through adulthood. Write the visit into your lesson plans, stay engaged with your class during the visit (by walking around and helping students secure appropriate materials), and model how to find different materials. Better yet, ask the librarians to help. The more often you visit the library, the more your students will feel comfortable, and the more likely they will take advantage of the wonderful resources that are available. Inspire your students' families to do the same with the public library and the students' chances of becoming life-long readers are even better.

Once you better understand your students' needs and interests, look around for inexpensive books and other reading materials. Low-cost magazines and books are everywhere, yet many families and teachers never think to look for them. Challenge your students and parents to find things in common, everyday places like grocery stores, thrift shops, convenience stores, garage sales, and online. Book clubs are often very inexpensive and allow you to use points to buy books that your low-income students might not be able to afford.

Donations

Upon exhausting your limited budget, it is time to seek donations. People love to donate books, and students love receiving them. Simply put the word out there that you are looking for books to share with students. Tell everyone—

friends, family, neighbors, businesses, volunteer groups, social media, and even your own students. Creating a detailed flyer will help avoid any confusion and allow people to contact you with any questions. If you are concerned about being inundated with unsuitable materials, be sure to list qualifiers such as your target audience, suggested book topics, condition, reading level, publication dates, and so on. Before accepting any donations, make sure the donor understands that there are no expectations of how the books will be used once you receive them, noting that you may need to pass some copies along to others in need. This will avoid any misinterpretations from the donors if they follow up later on and expect to see their valuable donations on the shelf. The only condition of accepting book donations is that the giver must be fine if you are unable to use the materials and end up donating them to charity. In the "Reading Makeover Quick Tips" section of this chapter, we describe a number of sources for donations of books and other reading materials. When seeking donations, remember two important things:

- you need to ask
- have your class write a thank-you card for any donation

Don't let a lack of funding prevent you from upgrading your classroom library!

Personal Libraries

All of the donated materials you collect can be used to help students create their very own, custom-made personal libraries. A personal library does not have to be big, expensive, or fancy. For elementary school students, it can be as simple as a shoebox. Have students decorate their shoeboxes with their favorite hobbies and activities and then teach them to keep it freshly stocked with a few leisurely reading materials that they love. Explain the project to families and ask for their support. Be sure you encourage everyone to add any type of reading materials—books, magazines, comics, newspapers, Internet articles, and even eBooks. If you lack resources in students' primary language, what better way to interest them in books than to allow them to make their own books? After they write stories, songs, recipes, or dramas in their own language, they can work with a friend to translate the text. This is a great way to involve families. Struggling and reluctant readers may need extra help, so monitor them closely and help them as needed. Personal libraries give students a sense of ownership and increase their buy-in to reading, especially when given the chance to show off their creations to you or their friends.

The Game Changer

The Internet is a game changer. Anyone in the world with access to a computer and an Internet connection has access to more reading materials than everyone who lived before 1990. Do not forget that our goal is for students to read, read, and read, and then read some more. The Internet is often forgotten about or dismissed as a good source for reading materials, but the fact is that it is the biggest resource there is. With proper monitoring and some guidance, the Internet is a great way to get unlimited access to information on very specific topics that pique students' interests. Let us turn our struggling and reluctant readers into voracious information connoisseurs.

Beyond Books

Besides receiving book donations from businesses, we have found that many will donate materials they do not need. For example, since Danny's students did not have a rug to read on, he asked various carpet stores for any leftover carpets or samples that they had. Not only did he receive enough carpeting for his classroom, he received enough to carpet every classroom at his school and two others.

We have also asked for atypical items from businesses. For example, ask law firms if they would donate two hours on their copy machines. Most businesses will agree, especially if you are not soliciting their time or money.

Reading Makeover Quick Tips: Obtain Reading Materials

Danny founded a nonprofit that created school libraries in the inner-city school district where he worked. Then, he joined the Board of Directors of another nonprofit that organized over 250,000 student volunteers to conduct book drives that garnered over three million book donations. Along the way, he discovered a number of great ways to increase students' access to reading materials.

> ⇨ **Newspapers:** Newspapers are an excellent source for printed material. There is something for everyone in the newspaper, whether it is recipes for the cooks in the family, scores for the sports enthusiasts, coupons for the budget conscious, or stock prices for the financially minded. Most

major newspapers have education representatives who will arrange for each student to receive free newspapers delivered to your school each week (see http://nieonline.com/). In addition, these representatives usually provide packets of lesson-planning ideas and ways for teachers to incorporate newspapers into their curricula. Check out any popular breakfast meeting place and there is usually a row of newspaper stands, including many free editions. Why not grab a stack to share with your students? Better yet, why not make friends with someone at your local newspaper and ask for "day-old" or later editions of newspapers? They work just as well.

- **Service Organizations:** Almost every community boasts a variety of service organizations, such as the Rotary Club, Optimists Club, Chamber of Commerce, and Lions Club. Churches, temples, mosques, and veterans' organizations like the American Legion are also good places to ask for book donations. We have been known to flash our identifications (like Joe Friday), informing potential donors that we are teachers who need reading materials for our students. People are usually very empathetic and are willing to help in whatever way they can.

- **Nonprofits:** A variety of nonprofit organizations specialize in providing books to teachers and students in need. Reading Is Fundamental (http://www.rif.org/), Reach Out and Read (http://www.reachoutandread.org/), First Book (http://www.firstbook.org/), and Dolly Parton's Imagination Library (http://usa.imaginationlibrary.com/) are among the finest. Public libraries and newspapers usually have lists of such organizations. For example, in Los Angeles alone there are over 800 registered nonprofit organizations that deal with literacy issues. All you have to do is to approach your helpful reference librarian and ask.

- **Bookstores:** Major book chains often offer up to 20 percent off on books for teachers, and many will donate damaged copies to teachers. Bookstores are also great for promotional materials. For example, many will donate promotional posters and book cardboard cutouts. We have received donations of *Twilight* posters, life-size *Harry Potter* displays, and *Magic Tree House* bookmarks. Again, get friendly with the employees at these places. Most will go out of their way to help you once they learn the resources they were going to discard are going to a good cause.

- **Thrift Stores/Salvation Army/Goodwill:** These stores have always supplied Danny with a ton of reading materials for free or at greatly reduced prices when he described the lack of resources at the schools he served. You'd also be surprised how far a handwritten thank-you card from your students can go with cementing long-term friendships with businesses.

- **Garage Sales/Businesses:** Most people at garage sales will donate or greatly reduce the price of books for teachers. Garage sales are potential goldmines. Remarkably, garage sales have been one of the driving forces behind our accumulation of reading materials. After we handwrite thank-you cards to folks for their kindness, we have been amazed how they spread the word among their own networks.

- **Post Office:** Whenever a person moves and leaves no forwarding address, the post office holds that person's mail for a period of time. Danny once asked his local post office if they would give him any unclaimed magazines, and they provided him with hundreds.

- **American Automobile Association:** Many AAA offices will donate used maps, pamphlets, and tour booklets to classroom teachers.

- **The Friends of the Library:** Almost every library has a Friends of the Library (FOL) program, and most FOLs hold annual book sales. Books that are not sold are often dumped because libraries do not have sufficient space for all materials. Most FOLs receive hundreds of *National Geographic* donations, and they are often glad to pass these along to teachers.

- **Junk Mail/College Info:** Danny used to get his students to telephone various companies and ask to be put on mailing lists. Soon, students were receiving loads of mail on a daily basis. Best of all, he called several universities and received a ton of free materials for students to read. A variety of offices are willing to part with printed items they no longer need.

- **Other Sources:** Think of local agencies that are willing to give documents to your classroom. For example, one teacher asked her Congresswoman to donate copies of bills and press releases to her classroom, and the Congresswoman even came to the class to read to students. In Los Angeles, Danny asked movie studios and independent producers to supply him with any scripts they did not use, and he received almost 20,000.

- **Make Your Own:** If you lack resources in students' primary language, what better way to interest them in books than to allow them to make their own books? After they write stories, songs, recipes, and so on in their own language, they can work with a friend and translate the text. This is a great way to involve parents and families, too!

- **Book Clubs/Affiliates:** When schools conduct book fairs, they earn points to purchase books for their schools. Danny organized affluent schools to donate their points to under-resourced schools. He also uses his website (www.lazyreaders.com) as an affiliate for Amazon. Anytime Danny's website readers purchase one of his book recommendations via Amazon, it donates up to 10 percent to reading charities.

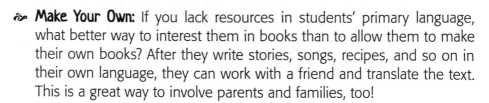

LESSONS LEARNED FROM MIKE & DANNY

Danny: My parents tell me that when I was around 18-months old I would sneak into their bedroom and start tearing pages out of books in their bedroom library. They would smack me on the hands and say, "Stay away from the books, Danny."

So, like any good son, I blame my parents for my early reluctance to read. (I'm kidding, of course!)

I always hated books when I was a kid. My father was a librarian, and I always hated public libraries growing up. They bothered me. Most public libraries I ventured into had uncomfortable furniture, distinct musty smells, and grumpy old ladies who insisted I lowered my voice; and there were always some shady characters from the streets who lurked by the book stacks, making other patrons uncomfortable.

My parents both read voraciously. Mom devoured mysteries—often finishing a 200-pager in a single sitting, while Dad's typical evening fare began with the newspaper, followed by a history book, then a glance at some bestselling novel at the time, with a dash of biographies, concluding with a massive volume on some world religion. As a family, we moved often when I was a child, and I remember having to haul box after box of my parents' numerous, heavy books. Conservatively, I would guess my parents had at least 5,000 books, not to mention the stacks that they supplied my brother, sister, and me. Note: My strength as a high school athlete was not enhanced by the weight room as much as by transporting heavy piles of *Sports Illustrated*, encyclopedia sets, and *Choose Your Own Adventure* books from one home to another. In contrast, seeing my inner-city students with limited access to reading materials was completely foreign to me.

The inner-city community where I taught had a population of over 100,000 residents, yet the only bookstore in the city was a Christian bookstore. Serving nearly 30,000 students, the school district reported library caches of approximately 56,000 books—less than two books available per student (more affluent districts typically provide a *minimum* ratio of 20:1, ten times the ratio of my district). I was appalled, so I founded my own non-profit organization that focused on securing more books in the district's schools. In less than three years, my nonprofit managed to receive over 80,000 book donations, more than doubling the district's reading coffers but still falling dreadfully short of the access to materials I had as a child.

Mike: Optimist International is a volunteer organization that "works each day to make the future brighter by bringing out the best in children, in their communities, and in themselves" (www.optimist.org). The local Optimist club that served our elementary school worked very closely with us during our Reading Makeover. Each year, they helped us collect thousands of books during our six-week book drive. I attended their monthly meetings to explain our progress and the impact their efforts were having on our students. I shared my appreciation through encouraging stories and the positive effects of their book donations and volunteer work. When they learned that the book donations were causing great excitement in our school, especially with our struggling readers, they really got excited to help, collecting as many books as possible. On the final day of the book drive, I would organize the books in huge piles all over the library and then schedule each class in the school to "come and get it!" I wish you could have seen the look on our students' faces when they were allowed to take a bunch of free books. You would have thought they had just won the lottery; they were so excited and thankful. They proved what research says: access to books is important (Miller 2010).

Conclusion

Having an abundance of high-interest reading materials keeps the concept of reading fresh and exciting for students, especially struggling readers. There are many different low cost and easy ways to surround children with books and create an environment where reading is important. Your struggling readers need your help to make it happen. You can do it!

Reflection Questions

1. As you were growing up, how much access did you have to books and other reading materials? How did this impact you as a reader?

2. Would you consider doing a book drive at your school? What local organizations could you approach to help?

3. What ways can you help low-income, struggling readers who may not have many books at home?

4. What other types of reading materials could you provide that are not too expensive? How can you get them in the hands of your students?

Chapter 4

Commitment: The Fourth Step to Reading Riches

Nothing extraordinary occurs through half-hearted measures. In this chapter we examine the importance of commitment to your reading program.

The Pope needed a heart transplant, and there was much concern throughout the Roman Catholic world. Everyone gathered outside the Vatican screaming and waving his or her hands. "Take my heart," they would shout. "Pope, take my heart!" The Pope did not know what to do, so an idea popped into his head. He asked everyone to please be quiet for a few minutes. Then, he told all of them that he was going to throw down a feather. Whoever the feather landed on, he would take their heart for the transplant. The Pope threw the feather down upon the people. Everyone was still waving his or her hands and screaming, "Take my heart, Pope!" This time, however, they were leaning their heads back and blowing the feather back into the air. "Take my heart, Pope!" they would shout, as they blew the feather. "Take my heart!"

How strong is your commitment? This chapter examines the psychology of commitment, the importance of commitment in successfully making reading a priority in schools, and suggestions on how to commit to developing healthy reading routines.

Getting people to commit to something can be tricky business. Then again, maybe it is as easy as persuading someone to agree with you on the tiniest point. Perhaps the optimal way to create a reading makeover is not to require every student to read 50 novels in six months; baby steps could prove more effective and longer lasting. As you will see in the anecdotes that follow, the *snowball effect* can produce great rewards and contribute to the development of a commitment habit.

Compared to World War II, an alarming number of American soldiers captured as prisoners of war (POWs) during the Korean War collaborated with their captors. Why? Had they been beaten? Tortured? Humiliated? Psychologists interviewed the Korean War POWs upon their return to the United States and learned that the Chinese Communists gained compliance not through brutality and intimidation but from a *lenient policy*: the Chinese got soldiers to comply with simple, seemingly trivial requests and built from there.

For example, after speaking with a prisoner for some time, a Chinese interrogator would convince a POW to concede that the United States is not perfect. Once the soldier complied, the Chinese might smile, offer his new American "friend" a cigarette and ask him to list ways the United States was not perfect. After writing a number of ways the United States was not perfect, the POW might then be asked to sign his name to the list and read it aloud to other prisoners. When fellow American prisoners tried to debunk the POW, he would find himself portrayed as a collaborator and begin defending his position. Edgar Schein (1956), principal American investigator of the Chinese indoctrination program in Korea, observed while only a few men were able to avoid collaboration altogether, the majority collaborated at one time or another by doing things which seemed to them trivial but which the Chinese were able to turn to their own advantage. Robert Cialdini (2009) notes how these actions were particularly effective in eliciting confessions, self-criticism, and information during interrogation.

To get someone to commit to a large task, the most successful persuasion technique is to induce him or her to commit to a small task first. Psychologists Jonathan Freedman and Scott Fraser (1966) asked housewives to place a large eyesore of a sign on their front lawns, urging passers-by to keep California beautiful. Half of the chosen housewives, however, were asked to put a small unobtrusive sign in their windows first. The result? The housewives who had agreed to the smaller request were far more likely to agree to stand the large sign in their garden—even if the two requests were made by, apparently, two totally unconnected people or even if the signs were about different issues.

Salespeople understand the importance of the small sale in paving the way for much larger ones down the road (known as the *foot-in-the-door technique*). Have you ever had your dinner interrupted by a telemarketer who asked you a series of innocuous questions that you inadvertently agreed with before finding yourself cornered? Salespeople understand that when a person says "yes" to even the tiniest purchase, that person is no longer a prospective customer: he or she *is* a customer.

Put another way, if you're serious about making over your reading environment, think about your bacon and eggs for breakfast. The chicken was involved in making the eggs for your breakfast, but it was the pig who was truly committed in giving you bacon!

We hope you are beginning to think about the basic steps you need to take to commit to a reading makeover. Do you think you could take some simple actions? Do you think these actions would benefit your students? Would you agree that these simple actions could lead to a significant impact on students' reading attitudes and aptitudes? Would you agree that this idea is so profound, that you should insist on investing in a copy of this book to give to every teacher and parent in the Free World? We know you think so!

Making Reading a Priority

Inspiring our students to become passionate, lifelong readers requires many different components, and at the heart of it all is commitment—by both students and adults. The way to get kids to love reading is to make it your priority in your classroom. You *and* your students need to make a commitment to becoming a classroom of readers. Commit in writing what your goals are, and pursue those goals ahead of all else.

In her book, *A Practical Guide to Prayer*, Dorothy Haskins (cited in Barnes 2008) tells about a noted concert violinist who was asked the secret of her mastery of the violin. The woman answered the question with two words: "planned neglect." Then she explained.

> There were many things that used to demand my time. When I went to my room after breakfast, I made my bed, straightened the room, dusted, and did whatever seemed necessary. When I finished my work, I turned to my violin practice. That system prevented me from accomplishing what I should on the violin. So I reversed things. I deliberately planned to neglect everything else until my practice period was complete. And that program of planned neglect is the secret of my success.
>
> (Barnes 2008, 205)

What is something in your life that is very important and requires a big commitment on your part? Is it your marriage; getting out of debt; parenting; exercising; or even getting through a long, seemingly never-ending school year with a really tough class? What motivates you to stay committed and fight through the difficulties day-in and day-out?

As we have seen in previous psychological studies, the quickest route to big commitments begins with smaller, more manageable commitments (Churchill and Lewis 1983). For example, research shows that while virtually all diet programs demonstrate moderate success in promoting at least some short-term weight loss, there is virtually no evidence that significant weight loss can be maintained over the long-term by the vast majority of people (Garner and Wooley 1991). You are not going to engage a reluctant reader by handing him a thick, classic novel and providing an hour of free-reading time in class each day. You need to position struggling and reluctant readers for success by beginning a program that facilitates simple, achievable tasks (e.g., read a newspaper article, memorize a funny poem, or write a song).

Have you ever watched a Hollywood movie on network television? You may notice that the first half hour has no commercials. Then, after a short commercial break, you enjoy another 25 minutes of the film without commercial interruptions. Soon, though, you may become frustrated as you notice commercials occurring more frequently and for greater lengths of time. What the network has cleverly done is enticed your interest to the point that you are unwilling to change the channel because you feel so vested that you do not want to miss the ending. We have to make reading the same type of experience for our students. When you observe a classroom of students who do not pop up out of their chairs the moment the bell rings because they want to finish whatever it is they are reading, you can get a pretty good idea that reading is a priority in that classroom.

Patience is key. Rome was not built in a day, and, similarly, a reading makeover bears more of a resemblance to Rome than to one of the many super-quick home renovation shows on television. Learning anything takes time. Some people grasp a task or concept within ten minutes, while others may take months or even years to fully understand something new. Some students are blessed with families and/or teachers who carefully, strategically, and regularly immerse them in reading. These students' journeys often result in superior reading abilities, increased passions and love for literacy, and overall successful academic careers (Krashen 2004). For the less fortunate, who missed out on those opportunities, reading can be torturously difficult, frustrating, and an overall negative experience. To become successful readers, these students need to have access to the thriving reading environment resources their more literacy-affluent peers encounter.

Creating a Thriving Reading Environment

When you exercise your body, you do not see results in a daily fashion. If you go to the gym today and work out for two hours, will you look thinner in the mirror tomorrow? Of course not. What about in a week? Probably not. However, if you were to take a photograph of yourself today, exercise regularly for the next three months and take another photograph of yourself at the end of the third month, do you think you would see any progress? Of course you would.

Measuring reading progress is the same. You probably cannot see much improvement in your reading from day to day, but if you examine its effects over an extended period of time, you are sure to see the benefits. For example, if you want to make the *Guinness Book of World Records*, time is needed to grow the world's longest moustache or to create the world's largest children's book or to become the world's most fit person. Becoming a better reader takes patience and discipline—good advice for teachers and parents to heed, as well.

Creating a thriving classroom-reading environment requires a lot of commitment from teachers. Here is a riddle for you to contemplate: What takes four to five hours a day and typically teaches children how to hate reading? Sadly, the answer is "school." Too many schools feel compelled to prioritize standards and accountability over interests and motivation. For example, following the

passage of *No Child Left Behind*, annual state spending on standardized tests rose from $423 million in 2002 to nearly $1.1 billion in 2008, a staggering 160% increase compared to less than a 20% increase in inflation over the same period (Vu 2008). Meanwhile, many schools have either greatly reduced or eliminated physical education classes over that same time period (Baker 2012). The emphasis on testing over play has become so prevalent and stressful to students that one testing company includes instructions on what to do with a test booklet when a student vomits on it (Ohanian 2008)!

Many teachers find themselves feeling handcuffed by mandates that appear to do everything in their power to *teach* kids how to read without considering how to *motivate* them to read. It has been said that schools provide practice and homes provide passion. Well, we do not think that is good enough, as many of our students over the years have come from broken homes. We cannot control students' home environments, but we can control our classroom environments. It is essential that teachers make a commitment to make reading fun for students in a classroom environment that supports reading achievement. When students are engaged in reading, their reading greatly improves. In fact, findings by John Guthrie (2001) suggest that reading engagement is so powerful that it cancels the gap in reading achievement when socioeconomic status is factored in with reading scores.

Tom Peters (2005) shared an observation attributed to Jimmy Breslin: "Every time I pass a jailhouse or a school, I feel sorry for the people inside (123)." Why is it that kindergartners will go to bed with their backpacks on, while eighth graders try to think of ways to get sick? What happened in those eight years to get those kids to hate school so much? If we are doing our jobs as educators, our students should be pounding on our classroom doors at six in the morning, and they should be in tears when the final bell sounds for the day.

LESSONS LEARNED FROM MIKE & DANNY

Mike: Our students need to study commitment as a character trait: what it is, why it is important, and how it relates to various aspects of their lives—both now and in the future. Far too often, we see adults in our society who easily give up on things, especially when they face a tough roadblock. As students examine real-life applications of commitment, we can help them apply the same principles toward reading.

In the alternative high school where I taught, dropping out is a daily temptation for many students. When talking with students, I like to share the story of my former classmate who would often quit things, especially when problems became too challenging. I explain how he would quit a sport when the season became too long, how he would quit his job after a conflict arose, or how he would break up with his girlfriend during a typical argument. Discussing my old classmate's mistakes opens the door for me to find out what is holding students back in their commitment to read better and more often. Students need to see the importance of commitment in overcoming obstacles, and I think it is important that we model commitment to our students. (We address the importance of modeling in greater depth in Chapter 5.)

Danny: An unusual characteristic of the Masai language in Africa is that there is no future tense. To convey a sense of the future, the speaker must use a complicated sentence structure. Even then, the meaning will not always be clear. While some would consider Masai primitive, I would argue the language is brilliant. It focuses clearly on the present. Sometimes, progress is made faster when we focus on the task at hand rather than let ourselves become overwhelmed with the enormity of any challenge. "Baby steps," I always advise students. "Let's enjoy the journey."

Getting struggling and reluctant readers to read often takes a nudge. It reminds me of the story of the wealthy Texas rancher who invited his entire hometown to his mansion for a barbeque. His house was decorated with the finest of everything, and his grounds were impeccable. However, he had filled his glamorous swimming pool with alligators that he had not fed in a week. When a guest asked him why, the rancher boasted to the crowd that he would give the deed to his ranch, $1 million in cash, or his daughter's hand in marriage to anyone who had the guts to swim the length of his alligator-infested pool. Never thinking anyone would be crazy enough to accept his challenge, he was amazed to hear a splash in the water.

The rancher and the rest of the guests stared in astonishment as a man swam his way feverishly across the pool, successfully evading the alligators. Everyone applauded and howled as the bloodied and exhausted gentleman emerged out of the other side of the pool. The rancher shook his head in bewilderment as he shook the

gentleman's hand. "I never thought anybody would be crazy enough to do that, son, but I am a man of my word," he said. "What do you want: the mansion, the $1 million, or my daughter's hand in marriage?"

"I don't want any of those things," the brave swimmer replied through gritted teeth as he cleaned himself off with a towel. "I want something else." The rancher was so impressed that he told the young man he could name anything he wanted. The gentleman looked around at the other guests and replied, "I want to know who the heck it was that pushed me into that pool!"

As teachers, administrators, and parents, we need to be committed to improving literacy now for our students, even if it means giving them a little push.

What Success Looks Like

Most people who have become successful have one important thing in common: they were passionate and committed to doing whatever it took to accomplish their goals. Think of any famous athlete, actor, entrepreneur, or anyone else who is highly respected in society. To reach their peaks, most had to start somewhere and work their way up. Have students research biographies about successful people whom they look up to. Ask students to find out what type of commitment was required for these people to achieve their goals and examine how they overcame any obstacles they faced. As students learn more about what commitment is and why it is important, they will have a better chance at applying it in their own lives, including in the aspect of reading.

When adults model reading, students better grasp the importance of reading. All students perform better at tasks where they have received guidance, but some students require intensive amounts of individualized instruction, with clear and repeated demonstrations of how readers and writers go about reading and writing (Duffy 2003; Harvey and Goudvis 2000). Left without adequate role models, many students are likely to continue struggling in their reading, leaving them frustrated and less interested in the activity (Allington and Cunningham 2007).

Having a positive role model is an important step. Another step is cultivating good habits.

No matter what the activity is, developing any type of good habit takes inspiration, focus, time, and commitment. Our students face many different temptations that can suck away their time and interfere with their ability to read on a consistent basis. Students, especially struggling readers, need help creating and maintaining structured reading routines. Here are a few tips:

SMART Goals:

- **S**pecific
- **M**easurable
- **A**ttainable
- **R**ealistic
- **T**imely

- ❧ Schedule consistent one-on-one reading conferences
- ❧ Help students set SMART reading goals that include routines
- ❧ Set students up to succeed by making sure they are taking small, incremental steps toward their reading goals

Establishing daily routines for activities that engage students in productive and motivating reading activities enhance opportunities to fulfill these tips. Scheduling daily free reading at home and at school helps students develop the habit of reading as a routine. Scheduling daily read-aloud time entices students to be interested in materials that they may not yet be able to read on their own.

What Conferring Looks Like

Conferring is the ongoing process of meeting with your students one-on-one and engaging in meaningful conversations about their reading experiences. Patrick Allen (2009) defines conferring as "...a verb meaning to consult together, compare opinions, or carry out conversations" (11). Conferring is a great way to determine your students' reading needs, likes, dislikes, wonderings, struggles, and successes. When you confer, make sure you have your students do most of the talking. Keep conversations focused on reading, but also allow time for students to connect what they read with their personal experiences.

When you first sit down with a student to confer, initiate your discussion in a way that quickly empowers him or her to take ownership in their reading experience. For example, you can begin by saying "Let's start with your overall thoughts and feelings about what you read. Did you like it? Why or why not?" A good follow-up question could be, "Tell me what you liked most about it." Framing an early question in this positive manor will help your student associate reading in the same positive light. Be sure to respect their opinion about things they disliked.

Avoid overuse of yes or no questions. A better alternative is to ask open-ended questions that require more complex answers. Get your struggling reader talking and engaged with plenty of nonverbal encouragement: smiles, good eye contact, and encouraging nods. Above all, make sure the student does most of the talking.

What SMART Goals Look Like

We know! It is not education unless you can come up with a clever acronym. Actually, SMART goals have been around for years in the areas of business and personal growth (Conzemius and O'Neill 2013). Just like driving a car without knowing where you are going or when you need to get there, you cannot reach a goal that you have not defined. Sit down with students and show them how to write specific goals. For example, "I want to be a better reader" is more specific than "I want to be a better student." Measurable goals show us how we know we have succeeded. For example, to measure what becoming a better reader means, a student may write that he or she wants to read 20 books by the end of the school year. Attainable goals should stretch students beyond their comfort levels. For example, if they already read 19 books a year, aiming for 20 is not much of a challenge. To determine whether a goal is realistic, ask students if they truly want to accomplish the goal. If they are doing something for anybody but themselves, there is a less realistic chance of the student accomplishing the goal. Goals are highly personal! Finally, goals need to be timely. A goal is a dream with a deadline.

What Incremental Steps Look Like

We are starting to sound like a broken record, but this is exactly what we remind our students constantly: Rome wasn't built in a day. It takes baby steps to accomplish grand things. For example, if we want to read 20 books this year (and the school year is 40 weeks long), we need to read a book every two weeks. If the average book is 300 pages, and there are 10 days in two school weeks, that means that we have to read 30 pages a day. We can offer students chunks of time in class to read (we recommend no longer than 10 to 15 minutes at a time). Make it into a game, and ask students how many pages they can read in that time period. If students say they read six pages, then have them calculate how long it will take them to read 30 pages at that pace. The goal is to encourage students to think about the simple steps it takes to accomplish big, seemingly unattainable goals. When they break down big activities into smaller, more manageable tasks, they begin to understand how anything can be accomplished with simple, consistent routines.

Commitment and the Reading Makeover

A successful reading makeover requires that you commit to changing the activities and behaviors that are not working. Change is necessary and inevitable in our lives. Granted, too much change can be unhealthy, but getting stuck in easy, ineffective routines can suck the fun and joy out of reading and cause kids to develop poor attitudes and bad habits. There is no reading panacea. One size does not fit all.

As Frank Smith (1988) says:

> Children don't learn to read from programs…programs can't anticipate what a child will want to do or know at a particular time. They can't provide opportunities for engagement…although some methods of teaching reading are worse than others…the belief that one perfect method might exist to teach all children is contrary to all evidence about the multiplicity of individual differences that every child brings to reading (220).

It is critical that you make a conscious choice to commit to whatever changes are needed to help your struggling readers. Create an effective plan to meet your goals, put your heart into changing what is needed, and then let your actions speak louder than your words. Neither of us has found many district reading programs to be sufficient or effective in producing engaged, excited, and effective readers.

In our experience speaking and consulting with thousands of teachers across the country, we have found that pre-packaged, "all-in-one," boxed reading programs cannot replace a curriculum that is tailored to the diverse needs of individual students. Reading programs that integrate a truly balanced approach to literacy are more likely to produce engaged, excited, and effective readers. We have found that truly effective programs empower educators to supplement programs with their own ideas, in much the way great chefs prepare recipes with their own added flair and spices. An effective reading plan examines the goals of the district and, considering the needs and interest of individual students, creates multiple routes to accomplish those goals.

Starting a new reading program can be so powerful and impactful for students, especially struggling readers. Many struggling readers, especially boys, like reading programs where they can earn objects and privileges that involve competition and offer a sense of purpose for what they are reading. Please do not misinterpret this: reading should always be the ultimate reward. Our goal is to make reading an activity that students always choose to do on their own for their own enjoyment. However, we have utilized a number of ways for students to "show off" their reading prowess—from wearing plastic necklaces with a bead representing every 20 minutes they read to graphs highlighting the number of books read to free passes to the library for students who read 30 minutes at home each day. Again, every student is different, so you have to come up with approaches that fit each student.

Depending on the program, beginning anew can also be overwhelming, daunting, and even intimidating for some teachers and librarians. It can take a lot of upfront work in researching, preparing, launching, running, assessing, and adjusting. We are already overwhelmed as it is, so why start something new? The answer is quite simple: anything that is new or unusual psychologically sparks interest. Godin (2003) argues that the only way to cut the hyper-clutter of products and advertising today is to innovate something new, unique, and remarkable—like a *purple cow*. Teachers, librarians, administrators, and parents need to understand that they are in the "edu-tainment" business. Variety and uniqueness are essential elements in attracting the interests of struggling and reluctant readers.

If you feel leery of starting something new because you are afraid of a long-term commitment, do not worry. Just give it a whirl and tell everyone that it is a trial. It is better to try something at least once compared to never at all. It is also important to remember the creed "all good things come to those who wait." Some approaches do not work the first time or the second time or the eighth time, but the breakthrough eventually occurs. Patience is a virtue, so keep your head up. Here are a few reading programs that we have been involved in over the years:

- Reading Buddies (older kids paired with younger ones)
- Book Clubs (weekly or monthly get-togethers)
- Rock the Mic (poetry, books, and music)
- Coffeehouse Night

Reading Buddies

Ever watch the television show *Little House on the Prairie*? One of the first things you'll notice is when the students are at school, they are all in a single classroom, and their ages and sizes vary greatly. It got us wondering, why are today's schools organized by age? That can be just as random as shoe sizes, especially in the early years when girls are generally more mature than boys. Cross-age tutoring is a great way to engage students. We have also found that by pairing older students with younger students, teachers are facilitating a situation where older students are seen as the more competent readers. And people who see themselves as more competent readers tend to be better readers (Beers 2003). Additionally, younger students have opportunities to see older students model more fluent reading. Whether one student reads aloud to the other or they read together, students have a chance to create their own shared reading experiences.

Book Clubs

We have organized all sorts of book clubs from book clubs for teachers, to grade-level book clubs, to theme-based book clubs. To model how reading should be a life-long social habit, teachers can share books (for example, teachers can exchange books by Mary Higgins Clark or Sydney Sheldon). We have organized book clubs where we challenged all students in a particular grade to read a particular book, author, or genre. Danny's highly popular Lazy Readers' Book Club (www.lazyreaders.com) promotes reading books under 250 pages. This club is based on the philosophy that the more books people read, the more encouraged they will feel about their reading competence.

Rock the Mic

Rock the Mic was an annual event Mike hosted in the library at his alternative high school. The concept of the event was similar to that of a talent show, except with a music and literacy theme. Students and staff would sign up to

demonstrate their love and commitment to literacy and music by either reading a poem, reciting an excerpt from a favorite book, or performing some type of musical talent like singing, rapping, or playing an instrument. A microphone and sound system was set up in the library, and on the given date, students would come to the library for an hour of entertainment by their peers. Aside from showcasing various forms of literacy, one of the goals was to simply bring students together and connect them with the library in a fun, laid back, and positive atmosphere. Students loved listening to each other speak and perform and appreciated how the event connected them with reading and the library as a great place to visit.

Coffeehouse Night

Have you ever had a student who basks in attention? Neither have we. If you do, however, find yourself teaching students who enjoy getting up in front of their peers and/or parents, encourage them to perform pieces that they have enjoyed reading. This activity stems from an event Danny used to host in his classroom called "Coffeehouse Night," where he and his students would dress up in turtlenecks and berets, invite parents to their classroom, serve their guests coffee, and deliver poems they had written on their "open microphone." You can do the same activity with students by encouraging them to recite poems, read short passages from books or other materials aloud, or sing songs.

Reading Makeover Quick Tips: Build Commitment

Students become committed readers through sound instruction and opportunities to read every single day. Alida K. Hudson and Joan A. Williams (2015) describe a framework for authentic reading based on the five components of reading workshop: time, choice, response, community, and structure. They report that in this context, students' motivation to read and ownership of their reading increases. Students learn commitment. Other ways in which you can help students build commitment are:

- Visiting the library every week
- Participating in book orders each month
- Letting kids choose what they want to read
- Scheduling guest readers regularly
- Dressing up like a character in a book
- Participating in character banquets
- Participating in summer reading challenges at public libraries
- Reading photo walls that feature photos of kids reading

Follow through! See if students are following their reading routines. If not, help them get back on track and adjust their routines or goals if needed.

Conclusion

It is critical to identify what causes students to enjoy or detest reading. No single reading program offers *the* solution. We are not interested in catching one fish; we want to catch as many as possible. Experimenting with different reading programs may help you cast a wider net that reaches more of your struggling and reluctant readers.

For more than 600 years, conquerors with far more resources at their disposal attempted to colonize the Yucatan Peninsula and never succeeded. Hernán Cortés managed this feat by uttering three words that would change the history of the New World. As his men marched to face their enemies, Cortés ordered, "Burn the boats." His men were left with only two choices—die, or ensure victory. And fight they did, successfully conquering Mexico. If you want to make your reading makeover to work, you and your students need to "burn the boats." Make the commitment to succeed, and never look back.

Reflection Questions

1. Why don't some of your students like to read? How can you make reading so enjoyable for them that they choose to do it on their own?

2. How can you create a reading program that meets the needs of all students while fulfilling your district's requirements?

3. How can you break down your large, audacious goals in reading into small, manageable steps?

4. What are some innovative ways you can make your reading program enticing to your students? What is your "purple cow?"

Chapter 5

Models: The Fifth Step to Reading Riches

An *effective reading makeover takes* a team effort. In this chapter, we look at ways to recruit, motivate, and train others to model positive reading habits to students, so they have multiple reading mentors.

An anti-drug television advertisement in the 1980s featured a father confronting his son about marijuana he had found in his son's room. "Where did you learn how to do this?" the father demanded. Exasperated, the son looked straight into his father's eyes and replied, "You, Dad! I learned it from you."

For better or worse, role models are powerful influences in students' lives. They need a "special someone" in their lives that can model what it means to be a reader. Anyone who is capable of displaying an energetic, positive attitude toward reading can be a role model reader, whether it is a parent, celebrity, or coach. What matters most is that students see people whom they admire reading. Teachers provide guidance, inspiration, and leadership, as our influence can profoundly impact our students throughout their entire lives.

Unfortunately, many struggling readers lack role models in their lives, especially positive ones that they can relate to or aspire to be like. Far too often struggling readers do not see their parents/families reading on a daily basis, or even at all, and all the research shows that parents are the biggest influencers possible (Trelease 2011).

The good news is that your struggling readers have you on their side. As dedicated and caring teachers and administrators, we often do not see the fruits of our labor. We care so much about our students, and we can sometimes feel like our efforts are in vain: unnoticed and unappreciated. Please, never underestimate the impact you have. The more effort you make, the more you reach out to help and the more you give it your all, the more it will help students. Even better news is that you are not alone.

Recruiting Reading Role Models

There are great reading role models at every school—you just need to find them and ask them to help. School administrators, teacher-librarians, reading specialists, coaches, specialist teachers, cooks, custodians—any adult in your building whom kids look up to—can be a reading role model. Remind these "recruits" why modeling is so important and how much it impacts students, and show your appreciation for their time and commitment. Have them read a book aloud or talk about their reading experiences (good or bad). If they had bad reading experiences, encourage them to discuss how they overcame their obstacles to reading. When students hear words of encouragement from someone they see frequently, they will have constant reminders of why reading is important. If needed, be persistent in asking and reminding these recruits about the need to help your struggling readers. Do not assume they are too busy or not interested. Most of the time, they just forget and need a gentle nudge.

Do not limit your recruitment to within your school's walls. Partner with local businesses and organizations to bring in guest speakers or readers. Have them describe to students ways that reading helped them in their personal and professional lives. When Mike did his reading makeovers, he constantly had members of the community visit, including business owners, nonprofit leaders, and even the city mayor. Danny's classes had a Mystery Reader every Wednesday. Students never missed school on Wednesdays because they knew at some point, a stranger was coming to read aloud to the class. Sometimes the guest was a friend of Danny's, often it was a parent of one of the students, and sometimes various members of the community also volunteered to drop by. When Danny could not find anybody to come read to his class, he would send two of his students to "arrest" another teacher to come read to his class while he read aloud to his or her class.

Peers matter, so partner with local high schools and middle schools. There are many high school and middle school groups that love to reach out and help the community such as sports teams, clubs, student councils, and many more. Connecting schools with each other builds a strong sense of community for everyone and helps reinforce the importance of reading. When students are consistently engaged in reading activities with each other, they gain a sense that reading is socially acceptable and a normal part of the classroom and school culture.

Squash any negative attitudes toward reading, especially with older students. Be strategic in setting up reading activities that cause students to get excited and confirm that reading fills a need they have. Have students share their thinking in other formats besides talking or writing; for example, use artwork, audio, video and multimedia presentations. Online collaboration tools, such as Google Docs, often have a "comments" feature that is a great way for students to collaborate electronically and help support each other. The more positive reading experiences students model with each other, the stronger their skills and attitudes will be.

Using Mentor Texts as Models

Mentor texts are any type of reading materials that serve as a teaching tool to help students learn a specific skill or concept. Mentor texts are great for writing, but they can also be used in any subject area and come in a variety of formats and genres: magazine articles, fiction, nonfiction, comics, online articles, newspapers, picture books, poems, biographies, and graphic novels. For example, if a teacher wants her class to learn about cause and effect, she could use the book, *If You Give a Mouse a Cookie* (Numeroff and Bond 1985). Another example would be studying image captions and section headings in magazines to learn about text features.

For the most part, reading is an isolated activity. Typically, we are simply looking at pages, reading silently and keeping our thoughts to ourselves. How can we share our reading thoughts and experiences with students? Think Alouds (Davey 1983; Wilhelm 2001) allow students to hear what models think about when they read. For example, put a star next to this paragraph if you talk to yourself. If you did not mark the paragraph, you are asking yourself right now, "Do I talk to myself?" As adults, we have tons of background experiences and thoughts that come into our minds. Letting students peek into our brains before, during, and after we read gives them a chance to experience texts on a much higher level. Sharing our thoughts, feelings, questions, struggles, frustrations, and ideas while we read helps students think critically.

Think Alouds work particularly well when built around student interests. For example, choose an important topic that intrigues your struggling readers. Next, suggest that you are thinking of buying a smartphone and need to figure out the best one to buy that fits your skill level, learning style, and budget. Go through the entire process out loud with students, sharing your every thought. Talk about the issues you are worried about, do the research with them, read things out loud, and verbally process everything. Write down your questions, problems that concern you, and ideas you have to complete the process.

Think Alouds should be a two-way street. After modeling how to think aloud, gradually release that responsibility on to students. Get your struggling readers to share their thinking just as much as you do, if not more. The more they share, the more likely they will take responsibility in their reading.

LESSONS LEARNED FROM MIKE & DANNY

Danny: One of the craziest things I ever told a class of young elementary school students was to write about their lives. They looked at me like I was from outer space. "I'm only six," one boy said. "Nothing has happened to me yet."

I insisted that things did happen to him, every day. Most authors get their ideas from everyday experiences, I explained. It dawned on me that in order to get my students writing about their lives, I had to share with them experiences from my own life.

Authors provide wonderful models, and I cannot get enough of good anecdotes. For example, I would tell my students that when I was their age, one of my favorite books was *Where the Wild Things Are* by Maurice Sendak. A librarian once told me that when Maurice was a little boy, his aunts and uncles used to come to his house every weekend. They would make tons of noise and leave his house a total mess! So the illustrations of monsters for his book were inspired by his aunts and uncles. When I shared stories like these with my younger students, they would giggle and share their own silly anecdotes. And that, I told them, is where we get the ideas for our stories—from our own real-life experiences. If we expect students to write, we need to model for them how to do it.

Students pay attention to everything we do. If we want students to read, then, we have to read. And we have to show them the strategies we use when we read.

Mike: There I was—a young, impressionable 15-year-old basketball player—struggling to stay in school and trying to figure out my purpose in life. Out of nowhere, like a bolt of lightning sent by God, Michael Jordan burst into my world, captured my heart, and inspired me in ways I never knew possible. I remember being amazed at how athletic he was and how he dominated games with authority and talent. He was unstoppable, and I wanted to "Be like Mike."

Even though my family was part of the "working poor" socio-economic class, my mom somehow scraped money together and helped me buy the very first edition, black and red *Air Jordan* sneakers. Their beauty, power, and the hope they promised hypnotized me. It did not matter how much they stood out from my school's ultra conservative bun-hugger uniforms; I wore them with pride and confidence. Lacing them up transported me into another dimension. I became possessed. I became unstoppable. I became Michael Jordan!

At the time, I had no idea how important it was for me to have a positive role model in my life. My mom must have known, which is probably why she bought me shoes that we could not afford. I did not realize how impressionable I was or that Michael Jordan was helping define my character and the type of man I would later become. It did not matter to me what color his skin was, how old he was, how far away he lived, or what his background experiences were. All that mattered was that he inspired me, gave me self-confidence, taught me how to work hard and motivated me to constantly improve.

Now, more than 30 years later, Michael Jordan's impact on me is still significant. When I face obstacles, fears or self-doubt, I think about the character traits that I obtained from him and I know I can make it through the tough times.

It does not matter if it is basketball or reading—everyone needs someone to look up to.

Reading Makeover Quick Tips:
For Teachers and Administrators

It is important to remember that no matter what you do, you are always a teacher and role model. There is strength in numbers, so teachers and administrators need to unite in their "battle" to convert struggling and reluctant readers to become participants in what Frank Smith (1988) refers to as the Literacy Club.

- Host evening parent/family workshops. For example, host a literacy night where parents come to the school library in the evening and are presented with information about the importance of reading and provided with inspiring techniques that they could use at home to help their children with reading.

- Post tips like those in the Reading Makeover Quick Tips section of each chapter in classroom and school newsletters.

- Use read-alouds to talk about and discuss ideas or situations from the text selection, create funny drawings on the board, ask tons of questions, and lead fill-in-the-blank games to ensure that students are listening.

- Show students your passion for inquiry! Explain the questions you ask yourself, the steps you take, and your determination to find reliable information.

- Model silliness—get out of your comfort zone! Sing, dance, create goofy drawings, do character voices, and pantomime.

- Talk to your struggling readers privately, one on one. As both of us had our own struggles with reading growing up, we have found that simply sharing our own trials and tribulations often provides inspiration for our struggling and reluctant readers.

Reading Makeover Quick Tips:
For Parents

Many parents of struggling readers also struggle themselves, especially fathers. If that's you, don't let a lack of confidence stop you! Be encouraged that you don't need to be perfect and that your children will learn more if you admit things that you struggle with, especially if you show determination. These quick tips are easy to follow and enjoyable for both parents and children.

- Read aloud, and discuss what you encounter.

- Let your kids see you reading and talk with them about what you're reading: summarize, share likes, dislikes, best parts, and so on.

- Do a hands-on project that involves reading. For example, reading a how-to tutorial to create a paper airplane, cooking, building or fixing things, conducting easy science experiments, and so on.

- Recruit other adults to help as reading models including friends, family members, and neighbors.

- Volunteer to help! Get in the classroom whenever possible and appropriate to meet teacher and student needs.

- Take your child to the library once per week and the bookstore once per month. Be sure to get something to read for yourself.

To paraphrase something Rev. Jesse Jackson once said, "Children need your presence, not your presents." In other words, the key to modeling is not tied to any one method. What's most important is that you are taking time to read to/with your child.

Conclusion

For centuries, no one thought a person could run a mile in under four minutes. Then, in 1954, a young British medical student by the name of Roger Bannister accomplished what had previously been considered an impossible feat. Remarkably, within six months, more than 20 other people replicated Bannister's achievement. In the following year, over 300 people managed to do it, and since then, over 20,000 people have recorded times below four minutes, including high school students. Before they attained their goal, however, they had to believe the task could be done. It only took one man to illuminate the possibilities to others.

In the same way, teachers, parents and administrators can serve their struggling and reluctant readers by showing them how to become better readers. When students see how others like them have succeeded, they develop a winner's mindset that will serve them well.

 Reflection Questions

1. How can we model good daily reading habits to students?

2. When reading aloud to students, how can you "think aloud" in a way that encourages students to think about their own reading behavior?

3. In what ways are you modeling reading to students now, and what more can you do?

4. How can you recruit additional reading models at your school?

The Power of Discussion: The Sixth Step to Reading Riches

When you attend a speaker's presentation, do you tend to recall all of the bullet points the speaker lists on the PowerPoint slides or the stories that are told? Better yet, are you more likely to remember a lecture or a chat you had with classmates? One of the most effective ways to remember information is to discuss it with someone else (Schank and Abelson 1995). This chapter examines the importance of facilitating ongoing discussions with students about the texts they read and to encourage students to consider readings more deeply.

Talking matters for learning. Although it's possible to think without talking—and to talk without much thinking—each can strengthen the other. Talking also provides windows into what students are learning. I want schools to be places of rich learning, and therefore I want them to be places of rich talk. (City 2014, 10)

How often do we engage students in discussions about the books they are reading? Too often, reading is a one-way proposition. We have our own interpretations of what we read, and we often fail to solicit the feedback of our

students. It reminds us of the little girl who had just finished her first week of school. "I'm just wasting my time," she said to her mother. "I can't read, I can't write, and they won't let me talk!" When struggling and reluctant readers have more opportunities to discuss what they read, they often become more excited about reading. The more you read, the better you get. The better you get at reading, the more likely you are to read.

Students who struggle with reading usually do not like to talk about it, either. Many have had different negative experiences such as being teased by classmates for reading slowly, criticized by parents for making mistakes or even embarrassed by teachers when called on in front of the class. As our students get older, the more negative reading experiences they encounter, the more likely they will avoid taking risks, disengage, or even shut down altogether. In most cases, struggling readers do not understand why discussions are valuable and relevant to them, nor do they realize how much these conversations can help them.

One day, a first-grade teacher was reading the story of the *Three Little Pigs* to her class. She came to the part of the story where the first pig was trying to accumulate the building materials for his home. She read, "And so the pig went up to the man with the wheelbarrow full of straw and said, 'Pardon me sir, but may I have some of that straw to build my house?'" The teacher paused, then asked the class, "And what do you think that man said?" One little boy raised his hand and said, "I think he said, 'Holy cow! A talking pig!'"

We want reading to hypnotize all of our students. We want them so engaged that they lose track of time and beg for more. Have you ever done an activity for five hours, and it seemed like it only took five minutes? Conversely, have you ever done an activity for five minutes, and it seemed like it took five hours? We want reading to be a mesmerizing experience—not the dull drudgery that often predominates school districts' scripted reading programs. Discussions are paramount to this hypnotic behavior. Effective conversations, when set up properly, can strengthen literary concepts, provoke higher-level thinking, and open doors to further inquiry and interest.

The culture of the classroom and social practices at school influence students' view of reading and their willingness to share their thinking (Warner 2013). It is our role as teachers to create a loving, respectful environment where students feel safe and are encouraged to share whatever is on their minds. We must educate both adults and students about what effective reading discussions look like in the classroom, throughout the school, and at home. We need to inspire our struggling readers to believe that reading is important and that discussions are a valuable part of the experience.

Trust Fall

You have probably heard of the "Trust Fall," an activity where you are standing on a platform a few feet off the ground, blindfolded, with your back to a small group of people—presumably people that you know. After the procedure is explained and the guidelines are clear, all you have to do is lean back, let yourself fall and trust that the people below will not let you splatter to the ground beneath and safely catch you instead. Assuming the fall is successful, trust is initiated and a bond is created with everyone involved.

For a struggling reader to open up and engage in a discussion, the student must *trust* that procedures will be clearly explained and guidelines will be established and enforced. Together with your class, create guidelines that engender trust—guidelines that include aspects of respect, listening skills, and engagement. Students must know that speaking up will not result in ridicule and embarrassment. On the contrary, we need to celebrate any risk-takers who want to share their observations with the group. Keep discussions positive, and act swiftly if guidelines are broken. Once trust is established and students feel safe from criticism, their engagement will increase and reading skills and attitude will improve.

Book Discussions and Book Talks

Find a partner. Ask your partner, "What was your favorite book as a child, and why?" Then, ask your partner about what he or she is reading, or any good books he or she has read recently. You have just conducted a Book Talk. A Book Talk typically revolves around people sharing their favorite stories or whatever they are reading. A Book Discussion is more like what Oprah does on her show, where everyone reads the same book and provides their reactions to it. Call these activities whatever you wish, but understand the two activities are different.

Book Discussions

An effective Book Discussion has various components that make it successful. These include:

- **Discussion leader**—The leader may be the teacher or a student whose role is to make sure that everyone is engaged and that everyone's voice is heard. The leader guides the discussion to ensure that the conversation flows smoothly.

- **Discussion guidelines**—Because everyone is expected to contribute to the discussion, good listening skills are evident throughout the group. Guidelines for participating in the discussion are helpful so that everyone adds to the conversation. These guidelines are designed to encourage students who are quiet or reluctant readers to share their thoughts. Furthermore, the guidelines help monitor the behavior of louder, more outgoing students who can easily overpower a discussion. Guidelines may be structured; for example, having students place a token on the table after making a contribution. At the end of the discussion session, some teachers find it useful to have a quick review of the strengths or limitations of the conversation: Did everyone contribute? Did we listen carefully to each other? Did we ask questions when we didn't follow another person's ideas?

Book Discussions and *Book Talks* are two activities that provide opportunities for students to share ideas about books they have read, have listened to in read-aloud sessions, or encountered in other contexts.

Book Discussions are organized, purpose-driven sessions designed to build students' comprehension through dialogue in which everyone has the opportunity to participate. During a book discussion, students talk about their reactions to the same book that they have all read.

Book Talks are informal conversations designed to enhance students' motivation and interest through presentation of intriguing ideas about the author or content of any book. During book talks, students talk about their favorite books or different books that they are currently reading.

- **Discussion questions**—Effective questions are an important element in the success of a book discussion. Good questions can deepen comprehension and inspire students to think critically.

When setting up a book discussion, select reading materials that are engaging and easy to talk about. Keep the atmosphere relaxed and light. If possible, mimic a typical book club by allowing food and drinks. Converse about different genres, formats, writing styles, fiction, and nonfiction. Be creative as you plan various formats so that students come to expect taking on different roles with different individuals: large groups, small groups, partners, friends, non-friends, or age/grade levels. As with anything, if the discussion is fun and meaningful, students, especially struggling readers, will be more interested and engaged.

Book Discussions are very effective in one-on-one, partner, and small-group settings. Whole-group discussions take great classroom management; otherwise, they can be counterproductive. Smaller groups provide more opportunities for readers, especially struggling readers, to share their voices.

Book Talks

Book Talks are another great way to engage struggling readers. They are designed to motivate students to read a particular book or books. The talks should be fun and compelling, similar to theatrical performance or an entertaining commercial. They should have a marketing approach with the goal to *sell, not tell*. They are not the same as conventional formal book reports, which can sometimes serve to distance students from reading rather than encourage them.

Administrators, librarians, colleagues, and anyone else can facilitate Book Talks, but it is important to keep them concise, fun, visual (less "talk"), and energetic, with compelling reasons why the audience would benefit from reading the book. They are a great way to showcase nonfiction, magazines, comics and any other type of reading materials. Student Book Talks are a great way to entice their classmates to read particular texts. Teachers should model how it can look and function, but they should get students engaged and encourage creative ideas. Finally, it should be noted that our students are *digital natives*, and most of them have grown up with amazing technology at their fingertips. Take advantage of their interest with technology and have them create video book commercials.

Book Talks should not be anything like traditional book reports that can sometimes turn students off to reading. Imagine going to the movie theater and watching a movie that you really enjoyed or hated. Is your first instinct to rush out to your car, find an old napkin and pen in your glove compartment, and rush back into the theater lobby shouting, "What was the *theme* of that movie? Anyone know the three main characters?" Book talks are the exact opposite of book reports.

Book discussions and talks are meant to spark conversations about books. The more people talk about books, the more excited they become about them. Increased interest leads to increased comprehension, which makes book discussions and talks valuable tools in our teaching arsenals.

Read-Aloud Discussions

Reading aloud provides awesome opportunities to engage in discussions before, during and after reading. By reading aloud, you have the power to pause at any time to share what is on your mind (recall the discussion of Think Aloud in Chapter 5), and also find out what the listeners are thinking. If your students are not used to you reading aloud and/or discussing what you are reading, prepare them before you read. Explain that you will be stopping to ask questions and discuss that not only do they need to be patient, they also need to be engaged. The more you have reading discussions with students, the more patient they will get and the better they will understand why it's important.

As you read, mix up your observations and questions. Sometimes, a simple question or observation can provide a much-needed break from the text, and at other times more complicated questions can help monitor comprehension and also spark creative and more complex thinking. Do not be afraid to discuss problems you are having as a reader. Maybe you do not understand what or why something is occurring in the text. Let your struggling readers "be the experts," and help you. Being vulnerable to students shows that you are authentic while giving them pride and self confidence.

Nonverbal Needs

Many struggling readers, especially boys, are more visual/spatial learners and have limited auditory capabilities. Their brains are wired in a way that too much talking and listening will result in auditory overload, causing them to become agitated or "zoned out." This is a common, undetected problem that occurs in many classrooms. Well-intended teachers over-talk and simply do not realize the consequences.

John Medina (2008), author of the *New York Times* Bestseller *Brain Rules*, states that, "Women tend to use both hemispheres when speaking and processing verbal information. Men primarily use one...These clinical data have been used to support findings first noticed by educators. Girls seem verbally more sophisticated than little boys as they go through the school system. They are better at verbal memory tasks, verbal fluency tasks and speed of articulation" (252). The good news, however, is that these problems can be avoided, including during book discussions. First of all, to determine a typical length of time for stationary talking and listening, a good rule of thumb is to limit the discussion to one minute for each year of the child's age. For example, only expect five year olds to sit and listen for five minutes or less, while 11 year olds can cope for 11 minutes.

Take a proactive approach and incorporate physical movement into the discussion. Keep a close eye on monitoring the body language of your listeners. If you see restlessness or sleepiness, have students get up and move to different areas of the room for another activity. If needed, do a quick "brain break" to help them continue the discussion (e.g., standing up to stretch, doing jumping jacks, standing up and repeating a phrase or two related to the topic being studied). Book discussions that involve writing, drawing, graphic organizers, acting, or any other fun movement make it much more fun, especially for those with special auditory needs.

LESSONS LEARNED FROM MIKE & DANNY

Mike: The strangest thing happened during my first year of teaching. Before I explain this bizarre problem, it is important to understand a little background about my situation at that time. I had just begun my teaching career. It was a profession that I knew I would enjoy but one that I was not "born to do," like so many of my colleagues. I started the year with an embarrassing secret: I did not think that I liked to read. Despite this secret, I was ready to inspire my class of 32 sixth graders. I asked a colleague for a read-aloud suggestion, and she gave me the recent Newbery award winner *The Giver*, by Lois Lowry (1993). Even though I was terrified at the length (179 pages of small print without any pictures!), I was excited to dive in and get my students to fall in love with reading. Secretly, I hoped I would join them in their enthusiasm.

As the story unfolded and the list of characters and events grew, the most bizarre thing happened. While reading aloud, I started daydreaming! It was the oddest thing. I would be reading something, even adding expression in my voice, and the next thing I knew, I was a few pages further along, but had no clue what I just read aloud. Embarrassed, I just stopped and asked someone in my teacher voice to "explain to the class what had just happened." Of course, I did not let on that I had basically fallen asleep with my eyes open. I covered it up by just "seeing if they were paying attention."

Now that isn't the strangest part of this story. My read-aloud daydreaming episodes continued, but I just credited it to the fact that I was a poor reader (which I was) who had a short attention span (which I did). Book after book, the same thing would happen until one day I realized that my daydreaming episodes stopped when I did any of the following things:

1. discussed things before I "fell asleep at the wheel"

2. walked around the room while I read

3. drew on the board

Years and years later, after learning more about the male brain, I finally discovered that I could only manage about 15 minutes of auditory information. Fortunately, studies show that this is about the norm for most people. Once I recognized this, I realized I was not just a poor reader who had a short attention span. My brain was wired in a way that was heavy on the visual/spatial aspects and light on the auditory processing. Those things may still be true to this day for me, but now I am armed to prevent it from happening.

Reading *The Giver* to my class that first year ignited a spark that started my passion for reading. Each book I read afterward provided more and more sparks until one day, "Kaboom!" I learned about gender differences in reading and my fire exploded as if it had been doused with gasoline (more on this in Chapter 7).

Danny: My seventh-grade reading teacher was Will Hobbs, who is now a best-selling author of several young adult books, including *Ghost Canoe, Crossing the Wire,* and *Go Big or Go Home*. Will was the person who got me interested in reading for the first time.

He had over 5,000 books in his classroom library, and he would let us pick out whatever books we wanted to read. At the beginning of class, he would tell us what he was reading, we would tell him what books we were reading, and for the rest of the 50 minutes we read. Whenever we would finish a book, we'd take the book up to Mr. Hobbs, and he would put down the book he was reading to ask us three or four questions about our books. If he was satisfied with our answers, he would give us a point. Any book up to 200 pages was worth one point; he would give us an extra point for each additional 100 pages we read. If we accumulated 25 points or more, we would receive an "A" in his class.

He used the single greatest strategy I have ever seen a teacher use to get a student interested in reading: he found out what interested me. Of course, I loved sports, and Mr. Hobbs made a point of coming up to me once a week and suggesting a cool sports book that he had just read that he thought I might be interested in reading. What do you think the odds are that I opened up that book? One hundred percent, and this has remained the case with all of the students I have worked with. Students might not read these book recommendations at first, but I have found by the fourth time I follow this practice with my students, they are bound to dive into the text. Why? There is nothing more significant than someone a child looks up to—a teacher, parent, coach, pastor, sibling, or buddy who says, "I was thinking of you when I read this. Check it out." Mr. Hobbs had stumbled upon such a simple strategy that worked wonders.

The other thing he used to do was conduct Book Talks every Monday. I think one of the reasons so many kids do not like reading is because they do not know all of the cool things there are to read. I imagine plenty of adults do not know all the cool things out there to read, either. So I love pumping students up by exposing them to a wide range of reading materials that fit their various needs and interests, from books about sports heroes or dinosaurs to lengthy chapter books or graphic novels with amazing illustrations. Talking about books the way people talk about their favorite television shows or sports teams is a great way to engage students in the wonders of reading. As Walt Disney said, "There is more treasure in books than in all the pirate's loot on Treasure Island" (Disney 2015).

Reading Makeover Quick Tips: Successful Book Discussions and Talks

- Set up class meetings. Despite intense academic demands, many of the best teachers we have worked with schedule 15–20 minute class meetings a few times each month for students to discuss any problems or concerns. Teachers who carefully control and facilitate these meetings create a trusting atmosphere and a strong classroom community.

- Add visuals to Book Discussions and Book Talks. Give graphical handouts that will help facilitate discussions and talks.

- Structure Book Discussions to be easy and meaningful. Do not emulate a boring assignment that generates a feeling like it is just busywork.

- Set up a school-wide program for Book Discussions and Book Talks. Meet as a group to brainstorm different reading-related activities. Then rotate your schedule so that everyone gets a chance to share and discuss books with each other. Invite parents and community members, and you will create a community of readers that extends beyond your building.

- Join your own Book Club! Model for kids, and tell them what it is like. The more students see adults reading, the more likely they are to read. Take photos.

- Whatever type of Book Discussion or Book Talk format you choose, always remember to make reading fun.

Conclusion

One of the best ways that we know to attract students to books is through Book Discussions and Book Talks. Don't worry about what you call them—that's educational jargon. You can call them peanut butter and jelly! What's important is that you understand the different functions. Book Talks are promotional campaigns that get students excited about books by allowing them to talk about their favorite books or whatever it is they are reading. They function a lot like the people handing out samples at a big box store: they want to entice you to try different books.

Book Discussions, on the other hand, operate in a different way. Think Oprah's book club or city-wide activities in which individuals are encouraged to read the same title and participate in discussions about the selection. Book Discussions based on a familiar title enable students to engage in dialogue, share their personal reactions and interpretations, and have deeper conversations about the content. Such activities might extend to consideration of other titles by the same author. The purpose is to build interest in reading through conversations that reveal how individuals have similar or different interpretations of the same content.

 ## Reflection Questions

1. What do you consider is the value of Book Discussions and Book Talks?

2. How do Book Discussions and Book Talks help entice struggling and reluctant readers to read more?

3. How can you integrate Book Discussions and Book Talks into your reading program?

4. When will you utilize Book Discussions and Book Talks?

The Mystery of Gender Differences: The Seventh Step to Reading Riches

Boys and girls are different in many ways—their clothing, toys, behavior, interests, and so on. In this chapter, we explore gender differences with regards to reading. We discuss our own experiences as male teachers and students and offer ideas on how to better meet the reading needs and interests, particularly of boys.

Sometimes boys do the darndest things. Almost a billion people have watched the viral video, *Charlie Bit My Finger* (HDCYT 2007). After getting bit the first time, three-year-old Harry purposefully sticks his finger back into the mouth of his one-year-old brother, Charlie. Only this time, Charlie clamps down harder and does not let go until Harry is almost in tears.

Why in the world would Harry want to take the risk of getting bit? Why does Charlie find it so funny? How do they both get over the problem so quickly? We could analyze many components that are observed in this short clip: bonding, social instinct, emotions, communication, and so on. The bottom line is that it is not always easy to understand why boys behave the way they do. Sometimes it is obvious that gender plays a role in why boys behave the way they do, while other times it is not so easy to tell. One thing is for certain: boys and girls are different.

For the most part, society recognizes and respects gender differences in most areas of our lives, from clothing and hair products to magazines and toys. The list goes on and on. We recognize behavior differences, too. Studies repeatedly show that boys are disciplined at a higher rate than girls in school. According to the U.S. Department of Education, "while boys and girls each represent about half of the student population, boys represent nearly three ot of four of those suspended multiple times out of school and expelled" (2014, 5). While these assumptions may or may not always be true, it is obvious that differences between boys and girls are recognized.

Boys' literacy skills have been a concern for decades, and many experts believe that we are in a state of crisis. According to the National Center for Education Statistics (2013), data stretching back to 1971 shows that boys have consistently underperformed girls on national reading assessments—by as much as 11 percent in recent years.

Why is it that, in the world of reading, we often fail to recognize that the literacy needs of boys and girls might be different, as well? Each student has his or her own personal literacy needs, but far too often they are lumped together for instruction with a "one size fits all" mentality. Think about these questions:

- How often do we clump students together into groups by the reading level?

- How often do we sort books by topics for boys versus girls?

- How many teachers, parents, administrators, and librarians have extensive professional development on gender-based learning?

- How often do adults change their behaviors to match the gender-based literacy needs of our children?

If we know that boys and girls are different, we must respect that their learning styles and literacy needs are also different. Understanding and respect should cause us to learn about those differences and change our behaviors accordingly. This chapter will examine how the reading habits of boys and girls differ and offer suggestions on how to address the needs of both groups.

Understand That Boys Are Wired Differently

Boys have different literacy needs because their brains are wired differently, and their bodies have many different hormones running through them.

Gender expert Michael Gurian discusses the important role of testosterone:

> When you understand that the right side of boys' brains is wired for spatials, mechanicals, and visual graphics, you see why sports are appealing to boys; why video games are appealing to boys; why hunting activities, whether in nature or in Laser Quest, are appealing to boys. They're all about visual tracking of objects through space. That's what testosterone does. It also sets boys up to be more competitive and aggressive; to punch someone they like and cause that friend a lot of pain then both have a good laugh about it (2014, 1).

So how do we address the specific needs of boys? In a study of the literacy practices and preferences of 115 adolescent students, Douglas Fisher and Nancy Frey (2012) found that by modeling and providing a choice in what students read, teachers created a reading environment where teen boys thrived. Providing plenty of reading materials that support your visual learners is a critical first step. Examples include comic books (print and electronic), magazines, nonfiction books with lots of photographs, graphic novels, and image-heavy web sites. Digital storytelling is also a great way to engage visual learners. Consuming and creating digital stories implements a wide variety of literary concepts. We discuss digital storytelling again in Chapter 8, when we discuss different elements as well as a list of possible tools.

Have students use writing and drawing to engage with reading materials, especially with text that is more challenging. Graphic organizers are also a great way to help visual learners organize what they are reading and thinking.

 LESSONS LEARNED FROM MIKE & DANNY

Mike: I will never forget one of the most influential moments of my entire career. It was during the first year of my elementary school reading makeover. I was attending a professional development session by Dr. Anne Goiran about boys and literacy in which the speaker described gender differences. Still secretly thinking I was not a reader, my eyes were suddenly opened to some fundamental differences between boys and girls. I had already been a teacher and librarian for over eight years, yet I did not know about some of these issues. How could that be?

The biggest thing I remember from that day was the concept that most boys prefer to read nonfiction on topics of their interest. That was the moment a light bulb went off in my head, and I suddenly realized that I was wrong about my self-image as a reader. Here, all along, I mistakenly envisioned that to be a "good reader," you must know and like every type of reading—especially novels, poetry, and classic literature. I never realized that my definition of a good reader was wrong. I did not know that "good readers" often just liked one specific type of material.

When I returned to my library that day, I looked at my desk and saw a handful of nonfiction materials that I loved to read. I saw my basketball magazines, a book about Colorado jeep trails, and a book that taught me how to use Photoshop. Here, all along, I thought I was not a big reader, yet in reality, I was a voracious reader. I just had more narrow tastes than many of my librarian colleagues.

My excitement quickly turned to anger. I thought about how many reading opportunities I had missed out on growing up. I thought about all the times teachers forced me to read things in school that I hated. I thought about how rare it was for me to read these things during school. And I thought about how my teachers (and parents) did not know about the unique reading needs of boys. "If my appetite for reading these materials would have been filled," I thought, "I would have done much better in all my academic areas!" That excitement, anger, and sadness are what started my mission to educate myself and everyone I knew about how to help our struggling boy readers. My mission began with a blog, www.GettingBoysToRead.com, and ended up becoming my first book, *Getting Boys to Read: Quick Tips for Parents & Teachers* (2014).

Danny: Can I give you a teaching tip? The vast majority of our struggling and reluctant readers are boys.

Boys and girls are different. Girls will read books about boys. Boys will not often read books about girls. The trick is finding books that match boys' interests (the same holds true for girls, by the way). For example, I once worked with a third grade teacher who insisted one of her students, Mario, hated reading.

"Give me an hour," I assured her. "I'll get him reading."

I was wrong. It only took me 20 minutes. The book I handed Mario is called *Just Disgusting* by Andy Griffiths (2002). No, not the Sheriff of Mayberry. This Andy Griffiths is a terrific Australian author who has written a lot of "important" books, like *Just Annoying* (2003) and *The Very Bad Book* (2014). Mario not only liked the book; he memorized the first chapter by the next week.

The first chapter is called "101 Really Disgusting Things." I cannot remember all of them, but some of Mario's favorites included:

- Dog poo
- Accidentally stepping in dog poo and getting it on the bottom of your shoe
- Getting dog poo on your fingers when you're trying to get the dog poo off the bottom of your shoe
- Eating a hot dog and thinking it tastes like dog poo and then realizing that it's probably because you forgot to wash your hands after trying to get the dog poo off the bottom of your shoe

That is how you get a boy interested in reading! Do not get me wrong. I think *Anne of Green Gables* and *Little Women* are wonderful books. However, if you want to attract a boy who is a disinterested reader to a book, the appeal of the "gross factor" cannot be understated.

Create a Low-Pressure Environment

In today's day and age, there is way too much negative pressure for students to improve their reading skills. Sure, focused intentional reading is important for growth, but in a world oversaturated with test preparation, many boys get burnt out with these intense reading requirements.

As adults, very few of us find pleasure in constantly reading things that are too challenging to decode or comprehend. Our passion in reading comes when we curl up on the beach with a great novel, smile after a book teaches us to build a tree house, or giggle at a silly comic.

Our reading comes easily, without stress or the pressure of a high-stakes, intense test to follow. Boys, especially struggling readers, need easy materials to build their reading confidence and help them feel successful as readers. Then they can tackle more challenging texts to ensure that they are meeting grade-level expectations.

Provide Engaging Literacy Experiences

William Brozo (2010) observes "that boys will become more engaged readers if they're exposed to and have engaging literacy experiences around texts of interest" (137). He maintains that teachers need to become familiar with and value boys' literacy practices outside of school in order to enable them to succeed with school-related activities. Recognizing that boys are drawn to the digital media and alternatively formatted texts (e.g., graphic novels and comic books) and that they thrive in an environment that provides for multiple modes of expression, teachers can provide experiences that will motivate reluctant readers. These experiences can be approached in a number of ways through the following:

- environment
- resources
- activities
- family involvement

Environment

A literacy-rich environment is essential to promoting reading, as research shows that students who come from richer home literacy environments perform better in reading (Clark and Hawkins 2010). Here are a few tips to make your reading environment more boy friendly:

- **Provide movement.** Children—particularly boys—should be allowed to move around while they do their work. Leg tapping, standing, and doodling while reading, writing, or taking tests—activities often seen as distractions—can actually assist many boys in their learning.

- **Create a "reading fort."** Ask boys to assemble a reading fort in your classroom with PVC pipes and cool-looking fabric. The hands-on process of assembling a reading fort gets their buy-in as long as you get them to agree with the purpose of its' use—solely for reading. Toss in a couple of beanbag chairs and cool refreshments, and they'll be lost in reading before you know it.

- **Set-up a "Magazine Rocks" display.** To make this display, find a prominent location and set up an enormous "Magazines Rock" poster with large text that is easily visible from a distance. Cut out the front cover of "boy friendly" magazine issues and staple or glue them to the wall. Under each cover, write a brief, one to two sentence summary of the magazine and then market the display by encouraging boys to take a look.

- **Get students outside.** Confirm that the school offers playtime in the yard (many new schools are being built with no playgrounds) and that even on bad-weather days students have free time outside. Research shows that kids learn better after recess (Jarrett 2013).

Resources

Interest drives reading, so it is critical that we make sure that boys not only have access to reading materials; they also need access to the types of materials that interest them. Here are a few ideas:

- **Use comic books and newspapers.** They count! Provide lots of different reading materials for students to read—not just books.

- **Teach boys about "banned books."** One of the things Danny often did with students was to promote a book to students and then apologize that the book was probably too tough for them to read. Then, he would say that he would make it available for check-out, and students always flocked specifically to those titles.

- **Study the lyrics to songs.** Check out a website that posts the lyrics to songs, such as www.lyrics.com, and find age-appropriate examples of students' favorites. Then, have a discussion about the songs. You should be aware that some of the lyrics contain inappropriate language and content. Make sure to preview all of the content before selecting lyrics to use with your students.

- ✌ **Provide students with "cliffhangers."** For example, you could read aloud a book up to a crucial moment, and then tell students that if they want to find out what happens, they need to read the rest themselves. You could also provide *Choose Your Own Adventure* books that allow students to pick how characters respond to events in stories.

- ✌ **Provide a variety of nonfiction resources** and encourage students to use those that appeal to their individual interests.

- ✌ **Promote unconventional reading materials** such as lists, photos, directions, instruction manuals, charts, maps, brochures, and so on.

- ✌ **Find great reading websites for boys.** A simple Google search for "book recommendations for boys" will turn up thousands of suggestions; for example, http://www.guysread.com/; http://www.boysread.org/books.html; or http://childrensbooks.about.com/od/toppicks/a/books_boys.htm

- ✌ **Schedule book fairs.** Many companies can provide book fair materials for your school and will do a good job of providing an array of books that are directed specifically to boys.

Activities

Here is a hodge podge of other ideas and activities we have used to boost students' reading attitudes and aptitudes:

- ✌ **Use writing to improve reading.** Circling things, drawing, and writing notes in the margins of books often make it easier for boys to comprehend what they read. If writing in books is not an option, have students use sticky notes.

- ✌ **Show interest in what students write.** When students allow you to read their writing, be there as a reader. If it is funny, laugh. React honestly and emotionally. If the student does not want you to share, that is okay, too. Trust takes time.

- ✌ **Use Skype for whole-class book talks.** Connect with authors or even other students and have discussions about books or other materials they are reading.

- **Have individual reading conferences with students.** One-on-one sessions show that you are interested in them as individuals apart from the group.

- **Create a secret QR code for a "book of the week."**

- **Provide plenty of "brain breaks"** that allow them to get up and move around.

- **Have students role-play favorite characters** from the books they read. Similarly, host a character potluck where students dress as their favorite literary characters and bring food items from books (e.g., "stone" soup, green eggs and ham).

- **Allow students to use creative formats for reporting on their reading** (so that you avoid traditional book reports). For example, allow students to create iPad book presentations with iMovie.

- **Encourage lots of different movements and voices** to get boys involved physically and verbally with a story.

Family Involvement

Parents/families are students' most important teachers. While boys may often seem aloof, they are usually paying attention when we are not realizing it. Here are some nonthreatening ways parents can encourage reading for their sons:

- Remind parents to look for easy, low-pressure occasions (a car ride, vacation) where boys might like to write. Parents might get boys notebooks that are unlined and encourage them to draw and doodle.

- Parents might also suggest boys use their notebooks as scrapbooks to collect stuff—photos, feathers, ticket stubs, and so on. Boys are notorious collectors. These notebooks could include weird facts, quotes, rock lyrics, lists, and so on.

- Hold seminars to train families in simple ways they can work at home with their struggling readers.

- Advise parents to consider waiting a year before placing their children in preschool or kindergarten. Kindergarten is much more academic today than it was 40 years ago. Experts agree that schools are asking five-

year-olds to do what six-year-olds used to do. Although opinions and school cut-off dates vary, some boys with a fall birthday may benefit from delaying school an extra year. Parents should consult their boys' teachers and even pediatricians for advice and direction before making a decision (Breheny Wallace 2014).

&smbat; Host a family literacy night to help encourage parents/families with their struggling and reluctant readers. Provide free reading materials to attendees.

Reading Makeover Quick Tips: Golden Rules for Working with Boys

Reading affects everything. Boys who struggle with reading often begin to question their abilities in other instructional activities. You can do a lot to help these students see themselves as constructive participants in school activities by keeping in mind these golden rules for boys:

&smbat; Get to know your students as well as possible so you understand their thought processes. One of the most powerful ways to excite students about reading is to personally hand them books that you thought they, in particular, would like.

&smbat; Acknowledge that every boy is unique with interests that are constantly changing.

&smbat; Be optimistic about boys' reading skills. Remind them that "Rome wasn't built in a day."

&smbat; Be enthusiastic. It's contagious.

&smbat; Encourage often. Boys respond well to compliments.

&smbat; Show boys that they have a sense of purpose when they read successfully.

&smbat; Acknowledge that boys tend to be visual learners.

&smbat; Accept that technology is your friend. Allow boys to read Internet articles and e-books.

&smbat; Remember that "shorter is better" when working with boys who struggle with reading.

Conclusion

Many children do not want to eat their vegetables, but it is still our responsibility as adults to encourage them to do so. In the same way, it is important for us to realize that there are some students who do not like to read. The vast majority of struggling and reluctant readers are boys. Boys and girls are different. It is important to realize, though, that with a little creative thinking, teachers and adults can find innovative ways that draw boys to read more. In this chapter, we offered a wide array of practical, easy-to-use strategies to encourage boys to read more.

 Reflection Questions

1. Why do you think boys, in general, are more reluctant readers than girls?

2. How do you encourage boys to read?

3. What are some ways parents, teachers, and administrators can help boys who are struggling and reluctant readers feel more comfortable and competent as readers?

4. What is the most effective way you have found to encourage boys' reading habits?

Technology: The Eighth Step to Reading Riches

Perhaps more than anything else in the past decade, technology has transformed the way we read and impacts the way we think about teaching reading. In this chapter, we look at ways to embrace technology and utilize it positively to grab struggling and reluctant readers.

Margaret Patrick and Ruth Eisenberg were residents of the Southeast Senior Center for Independent Living in Englewood, New Jersey. Both were accomplished pianists and spent most of their lives giving lessons to aspiring children. Not long ago, each suffered a crippling stroke.

Margaret Patrick barely survived. She spent months in hospitals and rehabilitation centers before finally regaining movement on her left side. Her right side remained paralyzed. She would often say in halting speech, "I am happy to be alive."

The wisecracking and amiable Ruth Eisenberg often laughed about that moment when she suffered the stroke and lay on the floor of her apartment undiscovered for two days. Ruth eventually recovered—but she still did not have the use of her left side, and she was confined to a wheelchair for her remaining years.

Doctors referred the two women to the center, where they met for the first time. They soon learned of their mutual love for the piano. One day they sat down at the center's ancient green piano. Margaret's long fingers moved back and forth over the left side of the keyboard. Ruth's shorter, stronger fingers carried the melody on the right side. They sat close together and leaned toward one another. Margaret's right hand draped limply around Ruth, while Ruth's left hand lay motionless on Margaret's right knee. Their first attempt was Chopin's *Minute Waltz in D*. It was truly a revelation to both. Since then they have developed an extensive repertoire, performing for countless senior centers, veteran's homes, and hospitals. They were featured on television shows and provided inspiration to all who knew them and heard them play. All of this was made possible by a little clever thinking and access to a tool they both loved (Cuthell 2004).

Broadening Our Definition of Literacy

During a reading makeover, thinking outside the box is important, especially in terms of how we define literacy.

> "Literacy" is not simply the ability to encode and decode print. [It is] the requisite knowledge and skills to send and interpret messages through multiple media and modes in local and global contexts... [C]hanges in communication design, function, and mode in our rapidly changing world...[require] constant re-design of our means and methods of local and distance communications, [and] re-think[ing] what communicative skills it will take to participate successfully in that world. (Hawkins 2004, 19)

As mentioned in our introduction, the essence of a successful reading makeover is to have the right mindset, to think differently, and to change our behavior to best support what our students need, especially our struggling readers. If our goals are to inspire students to read, write, and communicate effectively; to achieve academic success; and to be college- and career-ready to compete for jobs in the 21st century, then we must make sure our definition of literacy is broad enough to include a wide variety of reading materials in both print and digital format.

The process of reading and writing continues to advance at an extremely rapid rate and is much more extensive than the traditional methods of relying solely on reading books and writing or typing papers. Most of our students are digital natives and have been surrounded with technology-based "literacy tools" since birth. These fast-changing tools allow them to be innovative and consume and produce information publicly, privately, independently, and collaboratively. Like it or not, students are bombarded with many different literacy tools in their daily lives: text messages, social media posts, comments, tags, images, instant messages, emails, phone calls, video calls, face-to-face conversations, articles, books, ebooks, and thousands of different apps and online tools.

Choosing correct tools and knowing how and when to use them effectively are vital to compete in today's fast-paced, information-rich personal and work environment. "In the 21st century," describes David Warlick (2009), "literacy now includes a range of skills to find, navigate, access, decode, evaluate, and organize the information from a global network information landscape" (17). The problem, however, is that students need help learning these skills. It is our responsibility as adults and teachers to make sure they do.

Embracing Technology

"Technology has been a double-edged sword ever since fire," says renowned futurist Ray Kurzweil. "It kept us warm, cooked our food, but also burned down our villages" (Raymond 2014, 66). Still, that does not mean we avoid it.

The advent of affordable smartphones overwhelms millions of students each day in ways that many adults are unfamiliar or even uncomfortable with. Most students are immersed in an information-rich world that bombards them constantly with a new type of literacy, which comes to them in a wide variety of formats. These various forms of literacy can be used innovatively to our advantage to help students read better and more often.

> Today's students are often described as *digital natives* because they are part of the first generation to grow up with the new technologies: computers, video games, digital music players, cell phones, and so on. Marc Prensky (2001) contends that today's students "are all 'native speakers' of the digital language of computers, video games, and the Internet" (1).

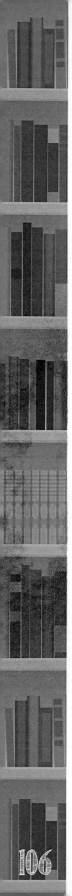

Far too often we see students sitting right next to each other and communicating by means other than talking. Have you ever heard this common complaint from a nearby adult, "They're sitting right next to each other—can't they just talk?" This seemingly impersonal, "less effective" method of communication is often considered inferior to the verbal conversation that adults are used to.

On the contrary, we can't assume that students are as tech-savvy as they may appear to be. Just because they have a smartphone, doesn't mean they know how to use it in a smart way. And what about students who haven't had access to technology like their peers? Perhaps their parents forbade it, couldn't afford it, or maybe the student simply lacks interest or desire in using technology the right way.

As adults, we can't expect to keep up with all the technology that our students use. We can, however, respect the communication techniques they engage in and not try to force our communication preferences on them. A better approach is to partner with students as learners and try to determine the best communication method for any given situation.

There are countless ways to engage our students in reading-based discussions that involve some type of recent technology. There are also steps to take to ensure students are safe and appropriate.

The biggest mistake many parents and educators make with technology is to simply avoid it. When we stick with old practices because they are familiar, we are really doing a disservice to our students. Embracing technology should be a never-ending mission for all of us. We should model to our students how to be brave, try new things, take risks, troubleshoot roadblocks, and learn from mistakes. Letting students be the experts is great, but it is even better when they see adults going through the learning process, too.

Do not get us wrong: we do not think technology is the panacea that answers all problems regarding how to best help struggling and reluctant readers (if we did believe that, this would be the only chapter in this book). Rebecca Miller (2014), Editor of Library Journal, puts it this way:

Any skeptics in your communities who think we live in a post-literate world enabled by voice-activated programs and multimedia learning should wake up. Just try to accomplish basic tasks without functional literacy skills—reading signs and prompts, keying search terms or answers on application forms, and so much more. As a nation, according to the National Center for Education Statistics (NCES), the United States falls well below par among other countries…Inside our borders some areas face illiteracy rates that should appall everyone working to build an equitable society. Philadelphia, for instance, has a shocking adult illiteracy rate that tops 50 percent, with low literacy plaguing two-thirds of the population. Worse, according to the NCES, we as a society aren't really gaining any ground on adult literacy over time, which points to a failure we must address in new ways. (139)

So how do we create students who are literate for the 21st century? Many schools across the country begin with the ISTE Standards. ISTE, or International Society for Technology in Education, is a nonprofit organization known worldwide for guiding educators to embed technology standards into their daily curriculum. Often directed by the leadership of wonderful teacher-librarians, ISTE standards play an important role in helping us define what it means to be literate in the 21st century.

Figure 8.1 ISTE Standards for Students

1. **Creativity and innovation:** Students demonstrate creative thinking, construct knowledge, and develop innovative products and processes using technology.

2. **Communication and collaboration:** Students use digital media and environments to communicate and work collaboratively, including at a distance, to support individual learning and contribute to the learning of others.

3. **Research and information fluency:** Students apply digital tools to gather, evaluate, and use information.

4. **Critical thinking, problem solving, and decision making:** Students use critical-thinking skills to plan and conduct research, manage projects, solve problems, and make informed decisions using appropriate digital tools and resources.

5. **Digital citizenship:** Students understand human, cultural, and societal issues related to technology and practice legal and ethical behavior.

6. **Technology operations and concepts:** Students demonstrate a sound understanding of technology concepts, systems, and operations. (ISTE 2007)

It's important that we don't see technology as an additional, separate subject, but rather as an integral component that is embedded in daily instruction throughout all subject areas. By adopting the ISTE standards into your curriculum, you can ensure that technology literacy is addressed school-wide.

Literacy in Our Pockets

According to the Ericsson Mobility Report (2015), 90 percent of the world's population over six years old will have a mobile phone by 2020 and 6.1 billion smartphones will be in use. When we think about tablets, computers, eReaders and other devices, the opportunities to access information are even more staggering. Think about the global implications of all these people with information available in their pockets, 24 hours a day. Think about all the different formats for how this information will be consumed. Text will be read and written, audio will be listened to and created, and video will be watched and produced. The question is, how capable will our students be in knowing how to find, filter, and use the information they need?

There are many different technology-based literacy tools available at our fingertips. Consumers reap the benefits of the ongoing fierce competition in mobile applications (apps) between Apple, Google, Amazon, and many other big players. Millions of free and low-cost apps provide countless opportunities for struggling readers to become literate in the 21st century. We just need to make sure we teach our students how to use them effectively.

Pros and Cons of Selected Electronic Devices

Love 'em or hate 'em, electronic devices are everywhere and in the hands of most students on a daily basis, especially as more and more schools implement BYOD (Bring Your Own Device) policies. There are thousands of devices to choose from with a plethora of reading opportunities available. Here are a few popular types of devices and some pros and cons for each.

Smartphones	
Pros	**Cons**
extremely popular and available to students day and night; instant access to information; becoming more and more affordable; can function as an eReader; becoming a global norm for information access	use can easily interrupt and distract students; hard to monitor when students misuse them due to small size; can be easily lost, stolen, or damaged

Tablets	
Pros	**Cons**
larger screens display more text and visual information, which make for a better reading experience; sharing is easy with partner/small-groups; have many capabilities and uses: Internet, video, audio, eBooks, camera, apps; many schools purchasing for student use on campus	can be more expensive depending on the make, model, and hardware features; bulkier than smartphones; don't support multiple users, making sharing more difficult; logistics in configuring: adding apps, performing updates, charging, checking them in and out, etc.

eBook Readers	
Pros	**Cons**
very affordable (most under $100); some have limited uses other than reading (which can help students focus); E-ink screens make text easier to read in daylight	some have limited functionality (no apps, internet, audio, video)

Laptops/Computers	
Pros	**Cons**
prominent in most schools; affordable	bulkier than smaller mobile devices; "old fashioned" or "not cool"

Many different devices such as computers, smartphones, and tablets feature eReaders. We must provide as many eReading opportunities as possible for our struggling readers, especially when traditional formats such as books, magazines, and newspapers do not always do the trick. Each device has unique pros and cons, and the key is to find the tool that does the best job inspiring a student to read.

Storytelling has been around since the beginning of time and still rules our world today, but no longer are we restricted to storytelling in the spoken or written form. Advances in technology have led to digital storytelling, making it easier and more cost effective than ever before. In addition to computers, smartphone and tablet apps add an amazing array of opportunities to help students create their own digital stories. Using a few simple techniques, some basic equipment, and a dash of creative organization, students can quickly share their story with an audience that spans the entire globe. Digital storytelling projects can be created with students of any age—from preschoolers to adults. Storyboarding and collaborating through audio, video, text, and images engage students with a nontraditional form of literacy that can open doors to reading and inspire a passion to learn.

Audiobooks are amazing resources that are underutilized with struggling readers. Too often, adults incorrectly think that listening to a book hinders a student's ability to read. Students themselves often refer to audiobooks as a form of "cheating." In reality, however, audiobooks provide fluency and comprehension that a struggling reader may not be able to experience when reading independently (similar to read-alouds). Audiobooks should not be the sole source of reading material a student is exposed to, but they should definitely be accepted—especially if the student enjoys them.

LESSONS LEARNED FROM MIKE & DANNY

Mike: As a kid, if I was curious about something, I faced various hurdles that would stop my hunger for information. I remember when I was about 10 years old and took apart an old radio that wasn't working. I hoped that by studying the internal components I could figure out the problem, fix it, and then crank some 80s classic rock. I recall being fascinated by the electrical components, curious about how it all worked, and hopeful to fix it.

My determination was short-lived because I knew it would be extremely hard to find information that would help me. No one in my family could teach me, we didn't have any books or magazines nearby, and the library was a long drive away. I was conditioned that the learning process was long, tedious, and practically impossible.

If I had a device back then with Internet access (along with the skills to use it properly), I could have found tons of information to fuel my hunger to learn. I could have found articles, videos, diagrams, photographs, sketches—even audio files. Being literate in the 21st century means having instant access to information and the ability to use it to satisfy our needs. Gone are the ancient, dark days of the Internet-less 80s. Our students are growing up in a world without borders—where a student in Africa with a laptop and Internet connection has access to more information than the history of civilization combined. The more successful experiences our students have in acquiring knowledge, the more they will be conditioned to keep asking questions and looking for the answers.

Danny: One of the most frequent questions audience members ask me at my presentations is, "Which is better, Danny: eBooks or traditional books?" My answer is always the same: "yes."

I am a guy who loves real books. I love to write notes in the margins, dog-ear pages, and quickly turn to the front or back of the book. I am also nosy and love to see what other people are reading. It makes for a great conversation starter. So many times I have walked into a bookstore looking for one specific book and wound up investing in ten or twelve books that caught my eye as I was browsing shelves.

That said, I understand a lot of folks' love affairs with eBooks. My wife goes nowhere without her eReader (sometimes she pays more attention to her Kindle than me!), and it is easy to see why. An eReader affords its owner the keys to any library, as any book or other printed source that is available for purchase on its systems is readily available. On long trips, I'd rather bring along my eReader than lug around the extra 20 pounds of books I bring with me. eReaders are great for nighttime reading, as text is easily illuminated and not imposing on others (again, my wife cringes whenever I read one of my old physical books beneath an actual lamp). Finally, now that I am getting along in years, I can truly appreciate the feature that empowers readers to enlarge font sizes on eReaders, too.

The important thing for teachers and parents to always consider is how to engage students. As previously mentioned, students today have access to more knowledge than the whole of civilization, using a pocket-sized device. Curiosity and the Internet can lead a person to solve equations and present solutions that were never thought of before. It is an incredibly exciting time, and one that can be used to nurture a real passion and lifelong affinity for literacy.

The Digital Divide

The digital divide refers to the gap between students who have constant access to technology and those who do not. Students who live in under-resourced communities or remote locations often do not have access to expensive technology that is comparable to that of their more wealthy peers.

We often think of the digital divide as a financial problem: a lack of computers and devices that can connect students to the Internet on a regular basis. While limited access to Internet-ready devices may be a serious problem among low-income communities, the bigger problem is students' lack of training on using the devices. As mentioned earlier, Internet access through smartphones continues to explode each year throughout the entire world, even in low-income neighborhoods. According to a recent Pew Internet research report (Madden et al. 2013, March 13), 89 percent of teens living in households with an income under $30,000/year have *daily* Internet access. So the problem is not necessarily access; it seems to be more about knowing how to effectively use the Internet as a tool for literacy.

Public and school libraries across the country provide training opportunities for students to learn 21st century literacy skills, but there are still not enough opportunities, especially for struggling students who live in low-income neighborhoods. It is up to schools to provide additional, after-school training so that both parents and students can grow in their mission to be lifelong learners. Aside from training, there are also financial resources available to help pay for technology services and equipment. For example, "Internet Essentials" is a program that Comcast (2015) initiated to provide affordable Internet access and computers to homes that receive free or reduced lunch programs. Additionally, since 1985 the Federal Communications Commission (FCC) has provided a program called "Lifeline" that provides a discount on phone service for qualifying low-income consumers to ensure that all Americans have the opportunities and security that phone service brings, including being able to connect to jobs, family, and emergency services (FCC 2015, August 28, https://www.fcc.gov/lifeline).

Technology offers limitless opportunities to learn more. Along with these opportunities, however, come areas of concern such as the mining and sharing of students' private data, students' lack of filters when posting photos and information online, and—through smart phones—getting contacted by adult strangers. Overburdened teachers forced into non-stop test preparation have very little time, if any, to focus on teaching students about online safety. Despite our busy schedules and curriculum demands, it is imperative to invest time in an ongoing manner to make sure students know what it means to be safe online.

LESSONS LEARNED FROM MIKE & DANNY

Mike: Part of my high school reading makeover involved my never-ending mission to inspire staff to embrace technology and apply innovative ideas to our new definition of literacy. Anne Coats was one of our English teachers who loved bringing her class to the library to read, research, and do technology projects. One of the things that made Anne stand out was that she was always willing to try new things with her students, especially skills that connected reading with technology. Anne knew that strengthening her students' information literacy skills would give them an advantage in the real world.

In the last few weeks before Anne retired, we collaborated on a multimedia-based research project where students had to collaborate together to research and develop an infomercial product that showcased what they learned during the previous eight weeks of the class. After 30+ years in teaching, you might think Anne would be tempted to coast through her last two months and take the "easy" road. Heck no! She was still taking risks with technology. She reached out to me with a request to have her students convert their written stories into video productions using the iMovie app on our school iPads.

Throughout the project, Anne's students used various forms of communication to collaborate, both with her and each other. The majority of their communication was talking face-to-face and also using Google Docs to collaborate, but they also sent text messages, connected on Facebook, and who knows what else outside of school resources. They researched, storyboarded, formulated their approaches, finalized their plans, and then got approval from Anne to create their videos. Anne hardly knew how to use the iPads or the iMovie app, but that did not stop her. She asked me to teach the class the basics, and then she had her students work together on the iPads to figure out any technical problems that arose.

On the last day of Anne's career, we both witnessed an extraordinary event. Our so-called "at-risk" students ended up creating the most amazing digital stories—ones that never would have happened unless Anne was flexible, resourceful, and willing to model how to take risks with technology and literacy. Her approach is an inspiration to us all—a reminder to embrace technology and try new things. And what a great way for Anne to end her career.

Reading Makeover Quick Tips: Innovative Technology Ideas ·

- **Model Your Technology Use**—Don't just sit back and let students learn technology by themselves. Roll up your sleeves and dive into the mix, even if you may not feel comfortable. Be brave and try one of the ideas below. Let them see you take risks in your learning.

- **Try Augmented Reality**—grab a recent copy of the Guinness Book of World Records, download their "See It 3D" augmented reality app, and use it with your struggling readers. Preface the experience with a creative story and you'll surely inspire a reading frenzy.

- **Integrate Technology with Project-Based Learning (PBL)**—Technology is an integral part of PBL. Guide students to showcase literacy in their PBL presentations in a way where they must demonstrate reading skills they used.

- **Try an eReader**—Read something with an eReading device that you haven't tried before. Take notes about the things you learned, questions you came up with, and discoveries you made. Then, share your findings with your students in a positive manner that gets them excited to try it themselves.

- **Create a Reading-Focused Makerspace**—Schools all over the world are establishing a special area in their building (often in the library) called a "Makerspace." This space contains numerous tools and materials that allow students to engage in self-directed, hands-on learning. Improve their experience by providing plenty of reading materials that relate to whatever they are making. See Mike's Makerspaces page for more information at www.ProfessionalDevelopmentForTeachers.com/ Makerspace.

- **Use Social Media**—There are countless ways to integrate reading with social media. Connect with an author on Facebook and tell your students about the experience, partner up with a colleague and participate in a literacy-related "Twitter Chat," or spend some time looking at and sharing book projects on Pinterest.

- **Schedule "Tech Tips"**—Talk with your principal to dedicate 10 minutes of every staff meeting to showcasing a connection between technology and literacy. Engage both your teacher "tech-nerds" who love to share, but also showcase a "tech-newbie" who can share literacy-related success stories. It's very inspiring when a "tech-newbie" steps out of his or her comfort zone to take technology risks that help struggling readers.

- **Tools for Digital Storytelling**—Check out all of the tools listed below for great storytelling ideas.

- **eBook Creation:** iBooks Author, MyStory, CreateSpace, StoryBuddy, Book Creator for iPad

- **General Tools:** Powtoon, VoiceThread, Prezi, StoryBird, Smories, PuppetPals

- **Images:** Animoto, Doodle Buddy, iPhoto, PhotoStory, Pic Collage, PicLit

- **Comic Book Creators:** MakeBeliefsComix, Pixton, ComicLife

- **Video and Audio Editing**: iMovie & Windows Movie Maker, Audacity

- **Script Editor:** Google Docs

Conclusion

Our students are inundated with technology and often lack the skillset to effectively find, evaluate, and use information in ways that they can benefit. Helping students become literate in the 21st century requires us to broaden our definition of reading to include media other than only printed materials. We must overcome any technology fears or obstacles and integrate technology into our curriculum in ways that can help students become literate with the wide range of information they will encounter throughout their lives.

Reflection Questions

1. How are literacy and technology connected?

2. Why is it important to implement technology standards into our instruction?

3. What are ways that technology can improve student achievement and future success in life?

4. What fears and/or frustrations do teachers have that involve technology? How can we overcome them?

Chapter 9

Rewards: The Ninth Step to Reading Riches

In this chapter, we examine different reasons that we read and study the role of rewards in reading. We look at the difference between extrinsic and intrinsic motivation and how we can facilitate reading environments that promote reading for reading's sake.

At the village church in Kalonovka, Russia, attendance at Sunday school picked up after the priest started handing out candy to the peasant children. One of the most faithful was a pugnacious lad who recited his scriptures with proper piety, pocketed his reward, then fled into the fields to munch on it.

The priest took a liking to the boy and persuaded him to attend church school. This was preferable to doing household chores from which his devout parents excused him. By offering other inducements, the priest managed to teach the boy the four Gospels. In fact, he won a special prize for learning all four by heart and reciting them nonstop in church. Even 60 years later, the "peasant boy" still liked to recite Scriptures, but in a context that would horrify the old priest. For the prize pupil, who memorized so much of the Bible, was Nikita Khrushchev, who would become Premier of the Soviet Union.

The same Nikita Khrushchev who nimbly mouthed the words of the Bible as a child, later declared God to be nonexistent because his cosmonauts had not seen Him in outer space. Khrushchev memorized the Scriptures for the candy, the rewards, the bribes, rather than for the meaning it had for his life. Artificial motivation will produce artificial results.

Anyone can develop the reading skills of a student who already likes to read. The real trick is working with students who do not like to read for one reason or another. The question, then, becomes, how do you entice students to read if they do not like to read?

Inspiring students to love reading can require a great amount of determination, focus, and effort, especially for students who are under-motivated or resistant to reading. Taking the right approach and knowing which techniques to use or avoid is important in helping our students succeed. Students need to be engaged in ongoing reminders about why reading is important (the rewards) and how it will help them in their lives, both now and in the future. This chapter will investigate the use of rewards in reading and paint a broader picture of the true rewards reading can offer students.

Reading for Reading's Sake

Pizza Hut has sponsored the "Book It" reading program for many years. The program encourages students to read by rewarding them with free pizza. While we appreciate Pizza Hut's support of developing children's literacy skills, we would suggest they make a modification to the program. In our ideal "reading rewards" program, every time a kid walked into a Pizza Hut, the child would receive a free book. The difference is subtle but important: children need to feel motivated for reading's sake, not for some arbitrary reward.

If we want to create a behaviorist-based system—a Pavlovian system— where students only read when they are offered candy, extra recess, or some other tangible reward, we should only expect students to salivate for books in anticipation of the presents they will receive. We do not want to use bribery to encourage students to read. Rather, we want students to read because they find reading to be a rewarding activity in itself. To do this, it is essential that students understand why reading matters.

The Benefits of Reading

Most adults understand the importance of reading. We have been around long enough to see how reading comes into play in various aspects of our lives, from performing daily tasks at work to corresponding socially with friends. Each year that passed in our formal schooling, we saw the important role that reading played in our academic performance and how reading helped us solve problems. If we were lucky, we also learned what an entertaining diversion reading could be. The older we become, the more we see the enormity of how reading affects our everyday lives.

Many of our students have not been exposed to these experiences. Many of them hate reading because the reading materials have always been dictated to them instead of based around their interests. They do not like reading because it too often involves mundane exercises rather than stimulating subject matter. Or perhaps they just are not yet very good at reading, so they avoid it because they are tired of feeling stupid. Students who naturally question authority are not as easy to convince, especially if they are low readers or have not been exposed to enough materials that they find personally interesting. These students, more than anyone, need constant reminders from individuals who are important to them—peers, friends, parents, teachers—about the benefits of reading. They also need engaging conversations about reading that relate specifically to their interests, concerns, and needs (Layne 2009).

Struggling readers are constantly asking themselves, "Why do I have to read?" When students ponder this question, give them tangible examples of the rewards that reading can bring. Remember that students who are disinclined to read may not always be receptive to the benefits of reading that come with adulthood: the expectation of future rewards is something students often have difficulty appreciating. Consequently, when talking with students about the benefits of reading, try to keep in mind benefits that are immediately applicable to them. These students need to take the *LEAP*: Learn, Escape, Apply, and Participate. (After all, it's not education unless we come up with a clever acronym!) Remind students that reading helps them to:

 Learn. Since reading is heavily required across the curricula, students who improve their reading skills are much more likely to achieve better grades. Reading is a vehicle that allows students to develop and improve skills (for example, vocabulary, writing, or spelling). It is a vehicle for

improving their knowledge of things they already know about but would like to know more about. Reading also allows students to enhance their critical-thinking and problem-solving skills (e.g., expressing emotions, overcoming adversity).

- **Escape.** Reading is an excellent means of tapping student emotions as an entertaining vehicle (joy, sadness, anger). Students can read as a therapeutic exercise to relieve stress, cope with problems, relax, or take their minds off their concerns. It is also an excellent way to prevent loneliness or boredom. Finally, reading enables students to use their imaginations and follow their curiosities.

- **Apply.** When students can apply something they have read to their lives in a meaningful way, it justifies their effort and reinforces the need to keep improving. Reading can be used to help solve their problems, improve skills they care about, and make their lives better. Informed citizens are better citizens, and readers take a greater interest in all areas, from history to politics, religion to science. Reading empowers students to become citizens of the world, entrenched in their communities. Students can use reading to improve their health (e.g., learn more about eating right, exercising, or disease) and model healthy living. Students can set a course for their future by reading up on career tracks, societal needs, and income opportunities. Reading helps strengthen relationships to help students deal with situations, such as making new friends, dealing with bullies, or coping with new siblings.

- **Participate.** The more people perform an activity, generally speaking, the better they get at that activity. Reading is no different. Nobody likes to feel like they are a slow reader or bad at reading. Those who read more become more confident at reading.

By taking the *LEAP* into reading, struggling and reluctant readers can derive numerous benefits. By helping students see those benefits, teachers, parents, and administrators can more actively engage these students in reading.

Intrinsic Motivation

If we want to motivate students to develop a lifelong love of reading, the best approach is to help them reap the rewards intrinsically. Intrinsic motivation involves "engaging in a behavior because it is personally rewarding; performing an activity for its own sake rather than the desire for some external reward"

(Cherry 2014, 1). In plain English, we want students to have a good attitude about reading because they find it meaningful, fun, or interesting. We do not want students reading simply because someone else is pressuring them, or they want to win a fancy prize, or they yearn approval from parents, teachers, or peers. With an intrinsic-minded approach, we will have a much greater chance that students will internalize reading as something that they value. Author Daniel Pink (2009) describes intrinsic motivation as, "the desire to do things because they matter, because we like it, because it's interesting, and because it's part of something important" (1).

Students need a sense of control to internalize their reading experiences. This is why so many authors, researchers, and educational professionals emphasize the importance of letting students self-select their reading materials. Think about it: no matter what the task is, you will be more motivated if you are given control to direct what you will do. Once things are out of our control, we disengage because we feel a shift in responsibility and a sense that it is not our doing.

Extrinsic Motivation

Extrinsic motivation refers to "behavior that is driven by rewards such as money, fame, grades and praise. This type of motivation arises from outside the individual, as opposed to intrinsic motivation, which originates inside of the individual" (Cherry 2014, 1). Other examples of extrinsic rewards include stickers, points, food, bonuses, nice cars, expensive houses, gold stars, and so on. Now, there is no denying that extrinsic rewards can be effective. We have seen preschoolers light up when they get a shiny gold star. We have enjoyed writing this book, but we will enjoy receiving royalties from it even more. The question at hand is, what will be the long-term impact of this approach?

Extrinsic motivation has plenty of critics. Alfie Kohn (1993), for example, believes that grading is not only arbitrary, it can be a harmful learning deterrent to students. He argues that research has demonstrated three flaws to using grades as external rewards.

- **"Grades tend to reduce students' interests in the learning itself."** Studies have demonstrated that a "grade orientation" and a "learning orientation" are inversely related (Beck et al. 1991; Milton et al. 1986). Research has also shown that students of all ages display less interest in their schoolwork and learning when they are being graded.

- **"Grades tend to reduce students' preference for challenging tasks."** When the goal of the student is to receive the highest marks possible on an assignment, often they will gravitate towards selecting the easiest possible topic in order to achieve that high grade (Harter, 1978; Harter and Guzman, 1986; Kage, 1991; Milton et al., 1986). The increased anxiety to receive high marks often leads to students choosing the easy way out, rather than challenging themselves.

- **"Grades tend to reduce the quality of students' thinking."** Studies have demonstrated that students are less creative when faced with achieving high numerical grades. Students who were given constructive feedback rather than a specific grade, were often more creative. Additional research has shown that students experienced difficulty understanding a social studies lesson after being informed they would be graded on their memory of the information presented. Conversely, students who were told they would not be graded often recalled more of the information from the lesson. This was still true one week later, during a measure of rote recall (Grolnick and Ryan 1987).

Now, let us apply this to reading. Picture a struggling reader engaged for a long period of time reading an intense, difficult article on a topic he or she loves. After finishing the article the reader is overwhelmed with pride and self-fulfillment at accomplishing the momentous task. Then, his or her parent or teacher gives him an extrinsic reward like a candy bar or a cool video game. How does the student feel about reading? He or she likely feels excited for the bribe, and probably no longer sees the value in reading for reading's sake. Kids are not stupid: they know if they have to be bribed to do something, it is often not worth doing on its own. On the other hand, how do you think this student would feel if he or she read the article and was able to use some of the newly acquired language in a meaningful way at school or with friends? Now is there a more apparent value to reading and a reason to pursue it further?

LESSONS LEARNED FROM MIKE & DANNY

Danny: Remember the fence-painting scene in *Tom Sawyer*? Tom is a bit lazy and mischievous (a.k.a. "a boy"), and his Aunt Polly makes him whitewash the fence around his house on one gorgeous Saturday. The clever Tom, though, manages to convince the curious on-looking children that not only is it fun painting the fence—they should also pay him for the privilege. Twain (1876) makes an important point that I think every parent, teacher, and administrator would be wise to etch into their memories: "In order to make a man or a boy covet a thing, it is only necessary to make the thing difficult to attain" (163).

One of the most well-researched findings in the field of motivational psychology is that the more people are rewarded for doing something, the more they tend to lose interest in whatever they had to do to get the reward (Kohn 1993). When parents ask me how to reward their children for reading, I usually first tell them to give their kids candy. If that does not work, soda is a good idea—especially something highly caffeinated. And, if neither of those work, I have found giving a kid $20–$50 does wonders.

I am being facetious, of course. Don't get me wrong: I use plenty of extrinsic rewards with students, but I try to always make reading the reward. So, if students do a good job, I reward them with an extra read-aloud or additional free reading time. Sometimes I'll reward students with a "Fluffy Friday," where I encourage students to bring pillows to class so they can lay down while I read aloud to them. And when I want to give students a physical reward, I head to a dollar store and I find plenty of books, journals, and writing materials.

If the students do a really good job, we may even visit our public library. Probably my favorite rewards, though, are the sticky notes I leave for students praising their persistence and acknowledging their hard work. For example, "Niceysha—I am so proud of how much reading you have done this year. You are moving mountains. I love you. Mr. Brassell" or "Ephraim—You have improved so much at reading! I love how you pick harder and harder books. Tell me whenever you need help. I am so proud of you, and I love you. Mr. Brassell." I find notes and genuine, *specific* compliments are the best motivators. They certainly have worked with me over the years.

Mike: I know this sounds strange, but I love the smell of manure. Seriously, I really do. When I'm near a barn I stop, inhale deeply through my nose, and smile as memories rush to my heart like a bouquet of flowers. The wonderful smell of manure instantly brings me back to my childhood days, the farming community of Wisconsin, and the intrinsic rewards I gained through hard work.

When I was 12 years old my mom sat me down and said, "Mike, an elderly couple needs your help with a big job; they need your help removing horse manure from their barn." My mom sighed deeply, and with a look of sadness, she drew the picture in my mind, "Can you imagine those two kind elderly people working in that horse stall; sweating in the extreme heat, trying to lift heavy pitchforks of dirty, stinky manure?"

Through her detailed description, my mom built empathy in me. She helped me visualize, step-by-step, all the things that needed to be done. Before long I pictured myself coming to the rescue and doing whatever was needed to finish the job. My mom skillfully primed me with her wit and charm; she practically hypnotized me into making me believe it was my idea to help. My mom told me they would provide lunch and a few bucks if I could help them with this difficult task. When I asked if I had a choice, she simply smiled and said, "I know it will smell bad and be hard work, but don't you think this is something you just need to do?" I knew what her answer really meant: I better rest up because I was about to embark on the biggest job I had ever attempted.

When I arrived in the barn, I couldn't believe my eyes (or nose). There were two 12 feet x 12 feet horse stalls and a blast of stench that almost knocked me off my feet. The manure was at least 12 inches high and so tightly compacted it was like driving a pitchfork into a block of cement. It didn't take long to realize the enormous project that I had just committed to.

As I struggled through each layer, the smell became more and more unbearable. After four hours of back-breaking work in 100 percent humidity, I stopped for the day, not even half-way finished. I was furious with my mom and wanted to quit. She nudged me gently, reminding me why this job mattered to both the elderly couple and to me. To my surprise, she took us swimming that day after lunch to a nearby lake. Perhaps it was a discreet way to reward me, or maybe just an easy way to wash the horrible smell that was glued to my skin.

After the second four-hour day I was exhausted and determined to quit. When the morning ended and I saw my mom, I exploded with anger and resistance, "Mom, this job was a terrible idea, I want to quit!" Putting her hand on my shoulder, my mom replied with compliments about my effort and character—my hard work, bravery, and determination. This was not what I wanted to hear because I knew that it meant there was no way out of finishing this nasty job.

When the third, and final day came, a strange sense of positivity came over me, and I felt much different. I was no longer upset or discouraged. I knew I was about to finish the monumental task, and I felt an enormous sense of pride knowing that I stuck with it. Heck, I even got used to the hard work, and the smell didn't seem to bother me that much. I finished the job and received only $20 as payment. To my surprise, though, the money meant nothing, and I didn't even want it. The reward I felt internally mattered more.

Thanks to my wonderful mom, it was during those pungent days that I developed a strong work ethic, the appreciation of a good challenge, and the ability to succeed when I had the right mindset. My mom's balanced approach in motivating me was significant. The extrinsic influences like cash, food, parental pressure, and swimming played a small part in motivating me. It was the way she rewarded me intrinsically that made a lifelong impact on me—encouraging me with loving persistence and complimenting my character and strong work ethic.

So now, when I encounter a patch of manure, I smell valuable lessons, fond memories, and the sweet aroma of intrinsic rewards.

Persistence

Rewarding students for reading takes a delicate balance of love and persistence. As parents and teachers, there are some things that we simply must require of our students. We must be persistent that they attend school regularly, behave themselves appropriately, bathe regularly and brush their teeth, eat properly, and so on. Improving our reading skills and nurturing our attitudes toward reading should be added to this list of required activities. When adults consistently follow up in a loving manner to help readers improve and battle through the roadblocks, we send the message that reading is important and we care enough to make sure improvement happens.

Sometimes giving a gentle nudge is all it takes, while other times your engagement requires a more direct or serious approach. No matter what approach you choose to use, it is important that struggling readers hear reasons why you are being persistent. "I'm following up and getting on your case because I care about you and want you to enjoy reading" is a great way to communicate your intentions.

Students also need to feel an appropriate level of challenge. Reading cannot be overly challenging in terms of the difficulty level of materials or the duration. Students want challenges that they can accomplish, but they need people closely involved to set them up for success by mentoring them, monitoring them, keeping them accountable, and teaching them to get back up when they fall.

Strategic compliments are one of the best rewards we can give struggling readers, especially compliments that are thoughtful, come from the heart, and are well timed. Compliments are easy, effective, and help build confidence in readers. Shallow compliments like "I like your book" or "good job reading" can sometimes work but the best compliments are ones that are crafted in a way that builds the character of the receiving person. Give compliments that are based on behavior. For example, praise significant reading efforts, improvements, determination, risk-taking, and occasions that connect the student's personality and talents with reading materials.

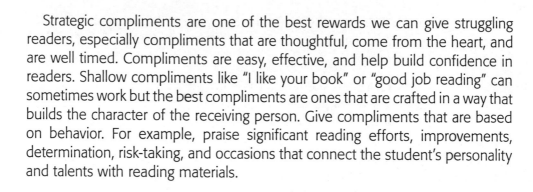

LESSONS LEARNED FROM MIKE & DANNY

Mike: I woke up one Friday morning by the buzz of a teacher librarian's text message: "Check the news," it read. "You're not going to like it." The news reported that $67 million in suggested budget cuts had just been announced, and—to my shock and disbelief—600 jobs were on the chopping block in our school district, including *half* of all teacher-librarians.

Not wanting to accept defeat, I quickly sprang into action and organized our teacher-librarian group. Two months later, we had a crew of parents, teachers, principals, and community leaders pleading with the school board to delay the budget cuts and ask for taxpayer support. The school board agreed to wait, and an intense nine-month grassroots movement began to educate our community about the situation and convince them to show support by raising their property taxes.

During the upcoming months, I knew our teacher-librarian group had our work cut out for us. I knew it would take teamwork and a huge commitment, not only from our group, but also from everyone else in our community who truly cared about our school system and knew what was at stake if we failed to get financial support. During those nine months, many friends and colleagues warned me that our voters would never pass the tax increase, especially as our economy had not yet recovered from the recession. Additionally, people would remind me that our voters did not have children in school or that the opposition was too strong. "It just can't be done," they would insist, incessantly. "It just can't be done."

I did not let that negative talk stop me. I committed to take action and do whatever I could to save our schools. I turned my RV into a roaming billboard and drove it all around town for two months. I launched a social media campaign on Facebook that reached over 500,000 people. I organized hundreds of people to march in parades. I even recruited hundreds of people to wave street signs and march door-to-door spreading the word that our schools needed help.

Election Day finally came, and—to the surprise of many—our voters approved a bill for a total of $138 million! All of our hard work paid off, the naysayers were wrong, and we were rewarded for all our hard work. Determination, commitment, and grit were required for us to meet our goal. We had to stick with it for a long period of time and make it through the tough obstacles and distractions.

If we want our students to develop positive reading habits, we must take action and say to ourselves, "We can do it!" The journey to learn how to read is not a sprint; it is a marathon. We need to dedicate ourselves as lifelong learners, open our minds, and be willing to change, if needed. Where there is a will, there is a way—that's what I say.

Reading Makeover Quick Tips: Reward Reading

To create lifelong readers, it is essential that teachers, parents, and administrators demonstrate the long-term benefits of reading in a variety of areas. While some extrinsic rewards may be a good way to encourage students, it is important to help students pursue reading for the sake of reading itself rather than for extrinsic rewards. Here are a few tips for implementing reading rewards:

- If you need ideas to remind students of the rewards that reading offers, check out the amazing booklists provided by librarians on their blogs or by companies such as book publishers or Amazon. You can find thousands of books available on just about any topic that you can think of, just by searching the Internet.

- Discuss the results of reading tests in a non-judgmental way. Justify a poor performance with concrete, specific reasons that don't insult students' character. Give them hope for improvement, make a plan to help them succeed, then follow up to make sure they do.

- Foster positive reading relationships—the more often struggling readers interact with people who love reading, the more likely their positive attitudes will rub off on them. This applies to peers, parents, families, teachers, and administrators.

- Give book prizes (reward students with actual books). Books are the best extrinsic motivators.

- Avoid using bribes to reward students into reading. They may work in the short term, but not in the long run.

- Validate what students like to read. It shows that you respect them.

- Avoid rewarding students if they haven't earned or don't deserve the reward. This is called the "over-justification effect." When students are rewarded for things that they already enjoy doing, their desire to participate in those activities decreases (Lepper, Greene, and Nisbett 1973).

- Avoid giving ongoing rewards that students anticipate. The reward will be much more meaningful if it is unexpected.

Conclusion

Reading should be the ultimate reward in itself. While we appreciate different efforts designed to attract reluctant and struggling readers to read more, research shows that these programs may do more harm than good. Once students understand all of the inherent benefits of reading, their motivation to read should be derived from their interest in learning more, relaxing, and utilizing reading to make themselves more productive members of society (Gagne and Deci 2005). The more we as adults validate students' reading efforts, the greater chance we have at ensuring these students read more often on their own. Try to facilitate an environment that encourages reading without resorting to common bribes. Remember: kids are smart! They know if you have to bribe them to do something that it is probably not worth doing on its own.

Reflection Questions

1. How do you reward students for reading?

2. What kinds of incentive programs can you offer your struggling and reluctant readers?

3. How can you challenge students to read without bribing them?

4. How can you convince your students about the importance of reading?

Chapter 10

Sense of Accomplishment: The Tenth Step to Reading Riches

In this chapter, we look at ways to promote students' reading by giving them a deeper sense of satisfaction. Highlighting students' growth is a critical way to illustrate their progress in reading. This chapter also considers ways to build confident readers based on the quantity and quality of resources that students choose to read.

Author, medical missionary, and explorer Dr. David Livingstone spent most of his adult life living in primitive conditions in Africa in the 19th century. While exploring in Africa, Dr. Livingstone once received a letter from some very well meaning friends. "We would like to send other men to you," the letter read. "Have you found a good road into your area yet?"

"If you have men who will only come if they know there is a good road, I don't want them," Dr. Livingstone sent in his reply message. "I want strong and courageous men who will come if there is no road at all."

When we were children we were told that things that were difficult were the only things worth having. Nothing feels better than when we accomplish something that is really difficult, especially when it involves overcoming fears

and obstacles. When a task takes a lot of time, hard work, and energy, we learn to dig deep and power through the challenges that pop up along the way. We use our prior knowledge and experiences to keep reaching for the light at the end of the tunnel. When we finally make it to the end, we look back at our journey with a great sense of pride knowing that we made it through and met our goal.

The Journey

Advanced, voracious readers know how a sense of accomplishment feels. They have been reading for a long time and have already made it through a variety of reading obstacles. They've encountered difficult texts many times before, and they know that if they stick with it and "fight through the tough times," sooner or later they will make it to the end of the tunnel. Their determination and stamina join forces with each passing success, gathering momentum for the next challenge. Fortunately, their challenges occur less frequently as they plow through more and more texts.

Unfortunately, struggling readers live in a completely different world. Their lack of positive reading experiences makes them feel like they are lost in the tunnel. Their reading obstacles are much bigger and come so frequently that the tunnel can seem more like a dark, dangerous sewer, with no hope for any light. Instead of plowing through, they often try to find the nearest exit as quickly as they can.

As caring adults, it is our job to jump in the sewer with our struggling readers and help them find the right tunnel. We must teach them how to overcome whatever inadequacies, anxieties, or fears they may have. We must inspire them to keep looking for the light at the end of their reading tunnel.

Confidence gets us through challenges and increases the chances that we will succeed. When we believe in ourselves, we are much more willing to take risks and try new things. Many struggling readers lack self-confidence in reading. They likely are embarrassed by one thing or another and may be shy or afraid to admit problems. One of the first things we can do is to better understand what these underlying issues might be. Having deep-hearted, trustworthy conversations will help to get to the bottom of any concerns that may not be visible from the surface.

The more positive experiences struggling readers have, the more risks they will take. As their confidence grows, you might see them engaging more often in reading, trying text that is longer, and eventually being more open-minded to selecting materials that may be out of their comfort zone. When we see struggling readers take risks and achieve milestones, we must celebrate them in a way that makes them feel proud of themselves: intrinsic rewards are the answer. In helping students develop a sense of accomplishment, we cannot overlook the positive contributions to the school and classroom culture that come as a result (Fisher, Frey, and Pumpian 2012).

It is important to help our students stay positive when they are struggling with self-confidence. We need to believe in our students and tell them why we care about how they feel. Struggling readers often feel guilty for taking too much time, making mistakes, or disappointing the people who are trying to help them. It is important that teachers, parents, and classmates are patient and caring and vocalize that everything is okay. Struggling and reluctant readers' perceptions of what others think can hurt their confidence and stop them from growing as readers.

Quantity

Excelling in any activity requires lots of practice. Think about how much effort it takes to master an instrument or a sport. Research first conducted by Anders Ericsson (1996) and popularized by Malcolm Gladwell (2011) in his book *Outliers* claims that the key to success in any field is, to a large extent, a matter of practicing a specific task for a total of around 10,000 hours. A big reason that advanced readers flourish is that they have put in many more hours than students who struggle with reading.

Many struggling readers come from "at-risk" environments. In spite of a variety of federal programs aimed at assisting these students, there has been little or no significant progress in helping the number of children considered to be "at-risk" of educational failure (U.S. Department of Education 2014). Significant differences in later reading achievement have been found between low-income and middle- to upper-income students, prompting an ever-widening gap that places low-income students at a significant educational disadvantage to their peers. Studies have found that limited opportunities with print are more likely to exist in the homes of low-income students and second language learners. Young students who have limited access to reading materials have been found to have less motivation to read, which negatively affects at-risk students' reading achievement throughout their subsequent schooling.

Early home literacy experiences have been shown to vary greatly, especially among different lower-income communities. One study of teachers across the United States revealed that teachers claimed nearly 35 percent of the nation's children are not ready for school, and 42 percent of the teachers said that the situation is getting worse (Boyer 1991). Many educators share the concern that many students, primarily those who are classified as being at-risk, are not yet "ready" when they enter school. It has been shown that many students simply have much more limited literacy experiences and opportunities than others, causing them to have a disadvantage upon entering school (Van Vechten 2013). In their examination of students coming from different economic backgrounds, Susan Neuman and Donna Celano (2001) found that while children in middle-income neighborhoods had multiple opportunities to observe, use, and purchase books few such opportunities were available for low-income children. These students also had much more limited access to quality books featured in more affluent daycare centers. In fact, researchers have argued that neighborhoods may play an even more significant role in students' academic success than their family income (Sastry and Pebley 2008). Research has shown that when a wide range of literacy materials in the home exists and parents read with their children, children read more (Krashen 2011). Increased exposure to books in the home has also been shown to lead to increased reading achievement at school. Essentially, those who have greater access to reading materials read more, and those who read more get better at reading. It leads to a "Matthew Effect" (Stanovich 1986) where the "rich get richer, and the poor get poorer."

LESSONS LEARNED FROM MIKE & DANNY

Danny: Jorge Luis Borges (1960) said, "I have always imagined that paradise will be a kind of library."

Well, when I was a kid, nothing turned me off more than libraries. See, my father was a librarian, and I often had to travel with my mom and younger brother and sister to the public library to drop dad off or pick him up from work. Public libraries always bothered me. The furniture was uncomfortable, the place smelled musty, and stern-looking elderly women always told me to be quiet.

Libraries freaked me out. So, contrary to what Jorge Luis Borges may have thought, I had it in my head that libraries were as far as I could imagine from paradise. I simply hated reading growing up. I took it for granted, though, that I had plenty of access to reading materials and two highly literate, passionate readers for parents. I may have not liked reading, but I was always good at it, if for no other reason than I was forced to read (which is probably why I did not like it).

The happiest day of my life—besides my wedding day—was when I received my doctorate. "From now on," I announced to my wife, "I get to choose the books." I have become an avid, eclectic reader because my interests are endless. I love learning about new things, which is why I loved being a journalist prior to my teaching career. Every story I was assigned to write meant a new opportunity to learn about a field I may have limited background in.

I read that by the time he was 30 years old, Teddy Roosevelt had read over 20,000 books. So that is why I started reading ten books each day. A lot of those books may be scratch-and-sniff or pop-up books, but I do tend to read about ten books each day. One of the reasons I created my book club, www.lazyreaders.com, was to encourage reluctant readers to read by recommending cool, short books. So that is why every month since 2003, I have recommended ten books: 3–4 adult level, 3–4 young adult level, and 3–4 children's books all under 250 pages so people have something they can read quickly. I figured that since the research supports the notion that the more people read, the better they get, I ought to advocate reading as many and as diverse titles as possible (Krashen 2004).

One of the biggest payoffs from reading lots of short books is it whet my appetite for longer works. So now, not only do I read plenty of magazines, comics, and screenplays, I often opt for the 800-page biography or 350-page mystery. I've managed to transition from trying to read as many different things as possible to also trying to read as many quality works as possible. Of course, I tend to read the children's versions of biographies, Classic literature, and Bible stories before trying out the original texts—whatever works!

Quality

Pierre Omidyar was a computer programmer who had the idea of auctioning off items on a portal of his larger personal website. One of the first items he sold was a broken laser pointer for $14.83. Flabbergasted, Omidyar contacted the winning bidder to ask if he understood that the laser pointer was broken. The buyer responded in an email that he was a "collector of broken laser pointers." Thus, the impetus for Omidyar's future company, eBay, was born (Hsiao 2015).

Who defines quality? What does "quality literature" mean? In many cases, what one person values as quality, another sees as trash.

We should not get too hung up on quality such that it inhibits a student's love of reading. It is important to recognize that discrediting what students like to read lowers their self-esteem as readers. Some teachers may scoff at students when they read things the teachers consider less adequate. We need to dispel that fallacy, as most of our experiences have shown us that it is highly unlikely that the best way you will engage struggling or reluctant readers is by starting off with classic literature.

Our job is to inspire students to want to read, and if they want to read nothing but comic books, where's the harm? If we really want to make sure students read materials of higher quality, why not build their "buy-in" by asking them to help define "quality reading materials." If we respect what students consider to be quality, their confidence will grow. Confidence in reading does not come overnight, and it is certainly not found on the pages of Moliere and Dostoevsky upon a first reading. Incidentally, students will tend to show interest in materials that their models show interest in, so if you want students to read Shakespeare, you need to read Shakespeare enthusiastically in front of them to spark their interests.

LESSONS LEARNED FROM MIKE & DANNY

Mike: My beer gut was out of control and something had to be done. With the help of a few close buddies, I embarked on an epic, chest-pounding, male bonding adventure that resulted in the ultimate physical accomplishment—completing the "Tough Mudder." This extreme adventure race involves a 13-mile, boot camp-style course that includes 22 challenging obstacles, the toughest of which involves getting shocked with 10,000 volts of electricity. Yes, it's insane.

Losing the beer gut and getting in shape were no small tasks, either. It took hard work, commitment, optimism, and encouragement from others. As a team, our goal wasn't to see how fast we could finish; we just wanted to complete the entire event and at least attempt all 22 obstacles. After six months of eating healthy and exercising, the beer gut was gone, and I was in good enough shape to compete in the event. The only obstacle that I was worried about was the "Electroshock Therapy" obstacle. I watched videos online and knew it would take a great deal of courage to willingly run through the 10,000 volts.

After three hours and 13 high-altitude miles of grueling pain, we made it all the way to the very end, where our electroshock therapy and finish line awaited. As expected, a lot of people came to their senses and went around the obstacle, skipping it entirely. When it was my turn, I paused and contemplated taking the easy way out. I realized how far I had come to get to this point, and I really wanted to accomplish my goal of completing all 22 obstacles. I took a deep breath, focused on the finish line, and sprinted as fast as I could through the water and dangling wires of pain. I dodged and weaved, jumped and ducked, and made it almost to the very end without getting shocked at all. But within five feet of the finish, it hit me. A loud zap and blast of pain hit me, starting from my right shoulder and continuing all the way down to my left foot. The bolt launched me into an acrobatic spin that resulted in a sprawled out crash in a thick patch of mud. I got up, shook off the mud and pain, and walked through the finish line with my head held high.

The sense of pride and self-confidence I earned from completing this amazing challenge had an enormous influence on me—much more than I ever expected. Now, years later, when I face a tough challenge, I think back to how I made it through the *electroshock therapy* nightmare. This monumental accomplishment planted a new level of confidence within my heart. Now, when a tough obstacle blocks my path in life, I think to myself, "I'm a Tough Mudder. I can make it through!"

Many of your struggling readers are facing the same monumental task that I did in the completing the Tough Mudder. For them, trying to read demanding materials can be very much like the electric therapy obstacle I faced. They need your help to make it through the long event, to encourage them to work hard and succeed— no matter how scary or challenging the obstacles might be. Accomplishing their reading goals will build confidence in them and create a sense of pride that will last a lifetime.

Reading Makeover Quick Tips:
Build a Sense of Accomplishment

People don't walk out of their mothers' wombs, and students don't begin their reading with James Joyce. We'd like to offer some "baby steps" to attracting struggling and reluctant readers to challenge themselves more with their reading.

- Most guys prefer short texts. That's why magazines, newspapers, and comics are so popular among boys who struggle with reading.

- Use creative strategies to build struggling readers' reading stamina. We have found that contests in the forms of number of books or pages read, minutes spent reading at home, etc. are great motivators for this. You can also keep "reading timelines" for students that show the evolution of text complexity they have encountered (e.g., from *Goodnight Moon* in kindergarten to *Twilight* in 6th grade).

- Morale is a big part of a reading makeover for both students and staff, especially in schools that are under close watch for program improvement. So keep a smile on your face and positive thoughts in your mind! Of course, we have had great success encouraging students by counting the number of books, pages read and minutes spent reading at home.

- When reading informational text, many struggling readers feel a sense of failure if they do not finish a whole book. However, most nonfiction books don't have to be read in their entirety. Readers may opt to read only the chapters they need. Share strategies for reading smarter, not harder.

- Make your struggling readers' successes your successes. Remember the story of the teenager who lost his contact lens while playing basketball in his driveway. After a fruitless search, he told his mother the lens was nowhere to be found. Undaunted, she went outside and in a few minutes returned with the lens in her hand. "I really looked hard for that, Mom," said the son. "How'd you manage to find it?" His mother smiled and pointed out that they weren't looking for the same thing. "You were looking for a small piece of plastic," she said. "I was looking for $150." We need to put our students on our backs and make their challenges our challenges.

Conclusion

In this chapter, we examined ways to support struggling readers by helping them feel a sense of accomplishment. By encouraging students to read more often and to even challenge themselves from time to time with more difficult readings, struggling and reluctant readers can greatly enhance their reading attitudes and aptitudes. We can make reading fun and challenging at the same time.

 Reflection Questions

1. How do you fill your students with a sense of accomplishment in what they are reading?

2. What role do the classics play in your classroom reading program?

3. How do you bridge the gap between so-called light fare (e.g., comic books, newspapers, or magazines) with what others consider to be more challenging (e.g., classic literature or poetry)?

4. How do you talk to students about books of different complexity? Do you degrade lighter fare or acknowledge its usefulness? When you read-aloud classic literature, do you present the material in an engaging fashion?

Chapter 11

Atmosphere: The Eleventh Step to Reading Riches

Successful businesses take pride in making sure their space is clean, organized, and inviting because they know how much the right atmosphere reflects the goals of the entire organization. In this chapter, we inspire you to create the right atmosphere for your struggling readers. We examine the physical and emotional components that will set the right tone and help create a setting that is conducive to reading—both in your classroom and throughout your entire school.

A city in the Netherlands had a problem with litter. The sanitation department tried doubling the littering fine and even increasing the number of litter agents who patrolled the area, but to no avail.

Then someone suggested that instead of punishing those who littered, they could reward people who put garbage in trashcans. A plan to devise a trashcan that could dispense coins when litter was inserted was rejected as too expensive. But it led to another idea: the sanitation department developed a trashcan that played a recording of a joke when refuse was deposited! Different cans played different kinds of jokes, and the recordings were changed every two weeks. Citizens went out of their way to put garbage in trashcans, and the streets were clean again.

Think of a rigorous or difficult activity that you consider fun. Maybe it's playing a challenging game or sport, memorizing a speech, or learning a new language. No matter what the activity, if the process is fun you will have a better attitude, learn more, and stick with it longer than if it was boring, frustrating, or stressful. What kind of environment are you creating for your struggling and reluctant readers?

Visit Seattle's World Famous Pike Place Fish Market, and you will see a shop full of fishmongers spending their grueling, stinky, 12-hour shifts stocking, selling, and packing fish. Sounds miserable, doesn't it? Well, these workers take pride in customer service, and they have taken tasks others may find dismal and turned them into a game. Their emphasis on fun, friendliness, attentiveness, and enthusiasm have resulted in "Fish!" philosophy videos and a program that has helped millions of students and adults all over the world see the importance of having fun in whatever we do (Lundin, Paul, and Christensen 2000). If a reading makeover is fun, our struggling readers will thrive.

Learning Atmosphere

Do you encourage your struggling readers to succeed? What are you doing to help your struggling and reluctant readers to reach their full potential?

As a boy growing up in Los Angeles, Jack Kemp lived for sports—especially football. Like many boys, he dreamed of someday playing professional football. Considering himself undersized for the local powerhouse college programs at USC and UCLA, Kemp enrolled at Occidental College. It was there that freshman coach Payton Jordan called Kemp into his office and confided that of all the people on the team, he believed Kemp had the talent to someday play professional football. Kemp went on to excel at Occidental and play as a quarterback for 13 seasons in the National Football League and went on to run as the Republican Vice Presidential nominee in 1996. Later, he recalled the encouragement he received from Coach Jordan, and soon learned that the coach had told each of his teammates the same thing! Miffed for only a moment, Kemp realized that his coach had made his teammates and him better by encouraging them all to struggle harder to reach their full potential (Allen 1989).

Important considerations in establishing a successful reading makeover are setting up an environment and providing activities that are attractive to struggling readers—strategies that can spur motivation in students to improve their academic performance. Alexandra Usher and Nancy Rober (2012) observe:

Some students are motivated by the promise of a job or the ability to see how things they are learning in class apply to the 'real' world. For these students, opportunities like service learning, expeditionary learning, or other alternative learning programs can help engage them in schoolwork. Other students will try harder to succeed academically if they are rewarded with participation in another activity they enjoy or can apply the academic lessons and skills to something they enjoy doing. For these students, extracurricular activities might provide the academic motivation. Lastly, some students simply need to view academic content through a different lens or interact with content through a media they are more comfortable with. In this case, video games, social media, and other new technologies may provide the means for teachers to motivate students whose minds have been shaped by the technology age. In each of these cases, nontraditional strategies can help increase students' motivation by making classroom work more interesting, helping students see the value in academics, enhancing their opportunities to feel autonomous and competent, and encouraging social reinforcement (1–2).

Clearly, creating an atmosphere where struggling and reluctant readers believe they will succeed is a necessary, though not sufficient, step in our reading makeover. Think about how much time students spend during the day in the same classrooms and in the evening when they get home. It is important that both spaces have a relaxed and reading-focused atmosphere. Consider these questions:

- What do students feel when they walk into the space? Does it feel warm and welcoming?
- Do students feel safe and respected?
- Do students feel a sense of ownership?
- Are students greeted each day with kindness and positivity?
- Is there a lot of love and laughter in the air?

In terms of physical space, how a classroom and home looks and functions also influences the reading atmosphere. We want our classroom libraries to be more appealing than Willy Wonka's chocolate factory. Consider all senses. Touch matters. If you are teaching young students, it is a good idea to walk around your classroom on your knees from time to time to make sure all reading materials are easily accessible. Make sure there is plenty of comfortable furniture for students to relax on.

Of course, the classroom library needs to be visually appealing, too. Provide lots of colorful reading materials ranging from books to brochures to magazines to trading cards. We want our classroom libraries to be so visually appealing that our students are constantly stealing glances, thinking to themselves, "I want to go read in the library!"

LESSONS LEARNED FROM MIKE & DANNY

Mike: Natasha was an English Language Learner in third grade who had just transferred to our school shortly after the year began. She couldn't speak a word of English and was crying nonstop the entire first few weeks after she arrived. Our school ran a program called "Each One, Reach One" where staff members were matched up with specific students who needed special attention. My principal explained Natasha's story to me and asked if I could take her under my wing. I embraced the challenge and became determined to help Natasha.

By that point I had already made great progress in our reading makeover by improving the look of our library, but I knew Natasha needed an action that would make her feel good about school and help her to fall in love with the valuable library resources that she so desperately needed. I wanted her to know that the library was a warm and friendly safe haven to learn. As she walked into the library for the first time I could see the fear and apprehension in her tear-filled eyes. Knowing our communication barrier, I knelt down, gave her a friendly smile, and then spoke the universal language that all students understand—the language of laughter. I showed her the cover of a hilarious book, *No David* by David Shannon and then I took her on a walk. We slowly walked around a set of computers that displayed students reading, we meandered past a group of students sprawled out on the floor devouring a magazine, and then we gently sat down on comfortable carpet near our collection of funny picture books.

For the next 10 minutes we laughed and laughed and laughed as we uncovered the hilarious and mischievous adventures of a scrawny little boy named David. After we finished the book, we both knew that everything would be okay for Natasha

To hear my principal share her version of the story, visit http://www. professionaldevelopmentforteachers.com/ new-esl-student-part3.

and from that moment on she cried no more. Natasha fell in love with learning that day and with some gentle guidance, she quickly became obsessed with a desire to read on her own. She came to the library daily (often more than once) and believe it or not, by the end of the year she was reading at grade level.

Natasha's success story was the result of a lot of factors. Perhaps the biggest one was her connection to a warm, inviting atmosphere that was filled with meaningful activities, funny books, and loving people.

Danny: I am a highly competitive person. When I became a teacher, I did not just want to be a good teacher. I wanted to be so good that the school would be renamed in my honor. I wanted the superintendent erecting statues in my honor throughout the school district. I wanted every other student at my school peeking through my windows and mouthing through the glass, "I — want — to — be — in — there!" All kidding aside, one of the ways I tried to create this type of engaging environment was through my classroom library.

To me, the classroom library is the Venus flytrap that captures students' attention and holds them hostage to the wonders of reading. As educators, we need to consider creating atmospheres that appeal to all the senses:

1. Touch: I began my career as a secondary teacher and discovered soon after teaching my little ones that it was a good idea for me to wander around the classroom on my knees from time to time to make sure that everything was accessible to my students.

2. Sight: Your classroom library has to be visually appealing. I wanted my classroom library to be so stimulating that my students could not keep their eyes off it all day.

3. Smell: Spray some Lysol or brew some coffee in your classroom so your classroom smells fresh and inviting.

4. Taste: Let students eat and drink while they read. I like to eat and drink while I read! What we are trying to do is create a sensory experience where students associate reading with relaxing.

5. Sound: Let students listen to music while they read, and let them choose the music. In my experience, whether you teach twelfth grade, seventh grade, fourth grade, or kindergarten, students will always choose music with lyrics like hip hop, country western, or pop music the first few weeks. But after a few weeks, I have found students realize they concentrate better when they read to instrumental pieces of music like jazz, blues, or classical.

Our goal is to create atmospheres that drive students to choose reading over any other activities.

Classroom Libraries

Since so many struggling readers have limited access to books at home, it's essential to immerse students in books that are close in proximity. Richard Allington (2011) observes, "Struggling readers need precisely what good readers receive—lots of high-success reading experiences" (43). A well-planned classroom library can ensure that struggling readers have such experiences. Classroom libraries provide students with instant access to needed materials, especially when visiting a school or public library isn't possible. A great classroom library has these six features.

1. **Quantity:** The more books or other reading materials, the better. At minimum, have at least 10 books per student. So if you have 30 students, make sure your classroom library has at least 300 books. I know some veteran teachers that have collected over 3,000 books for their classroom library!

2. **Quality:** Try to collect books on topics that appeal to struggling readers. Make sure the books have cool-looking covers and are in good condition.

3. **Student Ownership:** Give students opportunities to buy into the library by having them organize, label, and promote the collection.

4. **Organization:** Have your struggling readers organize the classroom library by placing books into bins or tubs and group titles by popular topics and genres, with colorful, easy-to-read labels. Booksource.com (http://classroom.

booksource.com) has a great free tool called Classroom Organizer that makes it easy to help check in and out your titles. This tool also has great reports that you can run to see which titles your students have been checking out.

5. **Variety:** Keep the collection fresh and stimulating by rotating titles in and out of the collection.

6. **Marketing:** Have students create signs and posters and then come up with creative ways to entice their classmates to use them to take advantage of the classroom library. Do Book Talks and connect activities and lessons with the materials in the classroom collection.

Sensory Features

Pleasant sensory factors can often add to the classroom atmosphere. Smell is important, so if there is an unpleasant odor lingering, try brewing some coffee or having an air freshener handy. Give students plenty of opportunities to eat and drink while they read. We like to eat and drink while we read, so why not let them? What we are trying to do is to create a positive sensory experience where students always associate reading with pleasure. Finally, let students listen to music once in a while, and let them choose the music. It does not matter if you are teaching twelfth grade, seventh grade, fourth grade, or first grade, music is important. In our experience, during the first few weeks students will always choose music with lots of lyrics like hip hop, country, or pop, but after a few weeks they begin to realize that they concentrate better listening to instrumental pieces like classical, jazz, and new age music.

Some students have sensory problems, so be sure to find out what works and what doesn't, and then teach them techniques to handle any sensory-related issues. Lots of reading-based activities and engaging discussions should fill the air every day. Remember: the right atmosphere creates the right attitude.

The Power of Laughter

If you have ever seen one of our presentations, you know how important laughter is to us. We used to tell students that the average adult laughs 15 times a day, while the average kindergartner laughs 300 times a day. "You have the rest of your lives to be miserable," we'll say. "In this class, we're going to laugh a lot." We both know how much fun learning can be when laughter enters the equation. Laughing causes our brains to release chemicals that stimulate organs throughout our entire bodies. Our stress level decreases and our attitude improves. According to the Mayo Clinic (2013), laughter improves our immune system, relieves pain, helps us get through difficult situations, and also improves our mood.

Laughter is contagious and brings people together. Robert Provine (2000) points out that laughter is primarily a social vocalization that binds people together. It is a hidden language that we all speak. It is not a learned group reaction but an instinctive behavior programmed by our genes. Laughter bonds us through humor and play. In other words, laughter is a good thing.

When you read or discuss books, look for any opportunity possible to laugh out loud. Fictional books are loaded with characters that do and say things that are funny. It is up to you to point these things out to your readers. Model by laughing yourself and saying comments like, "That is hilarious" or "I can't believe that just happened! That's crazy." The more you get struggling readers to laugh, the more they will feel connected with reading, and their happiness will help transfer toward a positive reading attitude.

Author Visits

Author visits can have a significant impact on your struggling readers. A good speaker will spark new interests, inspire positive attitudes, and motivate your students to read. Hearing successful authors describe their reading and writing journeys inspires many kids to follow suit and set related career aspirations and dreams. Bringing an author's "outsider perspective" into your building can also create a fresh reading vibe and provide a needed break from normal reading routines.

Planning an author visit is no small task: done well it can be an investment for your students and your school. To find good authors, start the process by teaming up with other members in your school community. Set your goals and then do your research to make sure the author is fun, engaging, and respected by other schools and organizations. The last thing you want to see is someone who is boring or ineffective as a presenter to groups of students.

The magic of an effective author visit happens in the weeks leading up to the big day. Properly preparing for the visit is essential and often overlooked.

Far too often, authors show up and the students have little or no background knowledge about them or the books they have written. Getting to know the author as much as possible will make a much more effective visit. Collect plenty of copies of the author's books far in advance so students can read and get to know him or her. Have students research biographical information, the author's personal story, and so on. Have students engage in activities that involve writing, artwork, and/or multimedia projects. Market the visit to the community. Send flyers, make posters, and spread the word on social media. On the day of the visit, make sure your students have good questions ready and do not forget to take lots of photos. Finally, be sure to send student-created thank you notes as a follow-up.

LESSONS LEARNED FROM MIKE & DANNY

Mike: Our school-wide instructional goal one year revolved around critical-thinking skills for both students and staff. As a member of our Instructional Leadership team, one of my responsibilities was to provide our teachers with professional development. For this particular goal, I approached our instructional coach and principal with an idea to set up an author visit.

We met a few times to organize the purpose and goals of the visit, and then we continued our collaboration online via a Google Document. We involved a few teachers, researched possible authors, and ended up hiring Patrick Allen, author of a few professional books including, *Put Thinking to the Test* (2008).

We shared our Google Document with Patrick and then Skyped with him so that he could design his visit according to our needs. We prepared our staff for Patrick's visit by reading his books and also sharing a few online articles that he wrote.

On the day of Patrick's visit, our teachers came to the library for his training and we engaged in a fun-filled, informative session titled, "Thinking About Thinking". We laughed, we learned, and most importantly, we left the training inspired to help our students improve their critical-thinking skills. Our teachers immediately implemented what they learned into their lessons and everyone appreciated the work involved to bring Patrick to our school.

Reading Makeover Quick Tips:
Create a Positive Learning Atmosphere

Mary Poppins said that for every job there is to be done, there is an element of fun. She showed the two children she took care of, Jane and Michael, how any activity could be made more enjoyable by turning it into a game. It is with that same attitude and spirit that we offer the following suggestions for transforming the learning atmosphere in your classroom.

- ✌ Don't pressure, judge, stress, criticize, nag, or bribe
- ✌ Have fun: fun = engagement = attendance = improvement
- ✌ Gauge students' capacity for endurance—don't push too hard
- ✌ Engage students by connecting reading with their personal needs and interests

Struggling readers may be reserved or try to lay low, but deep inside, like everybody, they want to be part of something. Make that *something* being a member of the reading community in your classroom.

LESSONS LEARNED FROM MIKE & DANNY

Mike: Taking a break from the real world is important, especially when you can visit an augmented version! When I speak to kids during author visits, I'll do whatever I can to make the experience educational, motivating, and most importantly fun. My favorite activity to help accomplish these goals involves using augmented reality technology.

For "augmented reality," I tell an amusing story, and then just at the right moment I take out my camera so students can see an augmented reality character pop right out of the pages of my book—as if the character were in the room right next to them. The reaction from students is amazing! They explode with laughter and cheer as if they won the lottery. Each time I've done this activity, smiles that can be seem from across the room. When my author visit is over, students—especially the struggling readers—become obsessed with reading any of the materials I shared, not just the augmented reality ones. Their interest level skyrockets because of a few factors:

- the nature of an author visit

- the nature of Book Talks and seeing reading materials that they like

- witnessing their peers get excited

- the "gee-whiz" factor of augmented reality

Ultimately, no matter what reading activities we do with students, when we make the experience fun, students will walk away with the right attitude.

Conclusion

Creating a fun, reading-focused atmosphere is vital if you want to help struggling readers. With a little creativity and teamwork, you can make a difference by organizing an effective author visit and building an elaborate classroom library that you and your students can be proud of. The way your classroom looks and feels can ignite a positive attitude toward reading and positively influence students' performance.

Reflection Questions

1. What is your learning atmosphere? Are you a thermometer or a thermostat? Do you simply take the temperatures of your students or do you set the temperature?

2. How do you help struggling and reluctant readers become more involved in their own learning?

3. How can you create an awesome classroom library?

4. What are you doing to promote joy and laughter in your learning atmosphere?

Chapter 12

The Brain: The Twelfth Step to Reading Riches

In this chapter, we examine how the brain processes reading and how these functions evolve over time. Trying to understand how the brain functions can be difficult, overwhelming, and even intimidating. Rest assured—in this chapter we cut to the chase and share some basic yet important concepts that will help you. We share brain-based strategies that will inspire you to try new things and learn more.

Children and adults think differently. Danny has known this ever since he was in kindergarten.

One day, Sister Roseanna asked Danny's class if they all wanted to go to heaven. All of the students raised their hands except for Hector.

"You don't want to go to heaven?" Sister Roseanna challenged Hector.

"Oh," Hector replied. "I thought you were talking about today."

Hector was right. Too often, we tend to see things from one point of view, ignoring other possibilities.

The brain is an amazingly complex and mysterious organ. Humans have been reading and writing for 5,000 years, and scientists still have several questions as to reading and brain function (Miller 2010a). As a society, we go to extreme lengths researching and studying the brain in hopes of figuring out how it works, impacts our bodies, and influences our lives. The more we understand the role the brain plays in learning, the better we can motivate and improve the reading experiences for our struggling students.

The Early Years

The foundational skills of reading develop at birth and are built around the brain's ability to learn and process language. Language provides the building blocks for reading. "The sounds we encounter in our immediate environment as infants set language acquisition skills in motion, readying the brain for the structure of language-based communication, including reading. Every time a baby hears speech, the brain is learning the rules of language that generalize, later, to reading" (Burns 2012, 1). Students who struggle with learning to read often lack a language-rich environment. There is a huge disadvantage for young children growing up in environments that do not include enough engaging conversations before they start school. Findings from a study of children's language acquisition involving adult language input, television viewing, and adult-child conversations reveal the following:

- Back-and-forth conversation contributed the most to the child's future language score (six times more so than adult speech alone)

- Adult monologuing (one-sided conversation, such as reading a book to a child without the child's participation) was more weakly linked to language development

- Television viewing has no effect on language development—neither positive nor negative (Zimmerman et al. 2009)

Reach out to your community and make sure parents with young children know how important two-way conversations are. Encourage them to talk up a storm with their children—with books and without.

Mike: During my years as an elementary teacher-librarian, I worked closely with the preschool through first grade teachers to help our students be prepared for reading. There was a never-ending concern that the vast majority of our students were not getting enough exposure to language in their homes—both listening and speaking. We noticed that parents were not reading books every night and that their children were not getting exposure to different literacy-related games and activities that should have served as the foundation to reading readiness.

Our students who were raised in nonverbal/non-reading environments were extremely behind their classmates who came from home environments that encouraged consistent literacy routines and activities. After full-day kindergarten was initiated, our first-grade teachers shouted with excitement after the first day of school when they discovered how much more prepared their students were. With input from teachers, I started hosting parent workshops in the evening to educate our parents and inspire them to create a language-rich environment at home. We provided free babysitting and sent home flyers and reminders in our school newsletters. We had an overwhelming response about these workshops. Parents felt valued and teachers appreciated the extra support.

Keeping the Brain in Mind

Brain imaging studies have shown how difficult and exhausting reading can be for struggling students. These students have been shown to use up to five times more energy than fluent readers when reading (Hempenstall 2006). Five times! It should not come as a surprise, then, that struggling readers often do not choose to read and may become actively resistant to the task. It's exhausting for them!

Hallie Smith (2014) provides a colorful presentation (an infographic) of the brain that illustrates its parts and how differences in the workings of those parts can affect reading behavior. For example, left brain activity is often less developed in struggling readers. This suggests that individuals may have difficulties making connections between letters and sounds. The part of the brain (occipital lobe) that helps us understand what we see may not be well-developed in under-achieving readers with the result that they have difficulty interpreting individual words or letters when they see them. Another part of the brain (Wernecki's area) stores vocabulary. Weakness in the development of this area may contribute to reading difficulties. Despite these variations in individuals' brain development, Smith advises that students can become successful with instruction that is intense, motivating, and frequent. Such instruction occurs in an environment that encourages inquiry, provides models of successful reading, and allows students to make choices about reading selections and activities (Fisher and Frey 2012). Think about how you can make your classroom's reading environment more engaging. Would you want to be a student in your classroom?

Who are our most struggling readers? Predominantly, boys are our struggling and reluctant readers, so it is interesting to note studies showing that boys learn differently than girls. Brain scans tell part of the story. In general, more areas of girls' brains, including the cerebral cortex (responsible for memory, attention, thought, and language) are dedicated to verbal functions. The hippocampus—a region of the brain critical to verbal memory storage—develops earlier for girls and is larger in women than in men, resulting in profound vocabulary and writing differences between boys and girls. In boys' brains, a greater part of the cerebral cortex is dedicated to spatial and mechanical functioning. So boys tend to learn better with movement and pictures rather than just words (Gurian and Stevens 2004).

Some learning environments and activities are antithetical to successful brain-based learning. Behaviors such as the following should be avoided at all costs:

- Stand-and-deliver teaching style in which teacher talk dominates and student silence is emphasized

- Static seating arrangements (e.g., rows) that inhibit (or prohibit) student movement

- Discipline that is characterized by ridicule, criticism, sarcasm, nagging, yelling, bribing, and threats

- Assessment that consists of pop quizzes with no follow-up about answers

- Teacher direction and control that is the norm with no opportunities for student choice and where only the "right answer" is acceptable

- Parents that are contacted only when the student is in trouble or is being troublesome

There are also biochemical differences between boys and girls. Boys have less serotonin and oxytocin (hormones that play a role in promoting a sense of calm) than girls. That can help explain why it is more likely that young boys will fidget and act impulsively. Leonard Sax (2006) observes that teachers may interpret such behavior as being defiant; however, it isn't, because boys literally have more difficulty sitting still and being quiet.

The point is this: educators need to consider learning styles, brain patterns, gender differences, and biochemical differences as they organize instruction to meet the needs and interests of the students (Zamosky 2011).

Creating a Multi-Sensory Environment

Sensory integration refers to the brain's ability to collect information that our body receives through our five senses (smell, taste, touch, sight, and sound) and process it in a way that is helpful to our needs. Too often, struggling readers get overwhelmed with one sense or another and if the anxiety is not handled quickly and properly, it can lead to different degrees of behavioral meltdown. For an optimal educational experience, it is best to involve activities that are multi-sensory. Here are some quick tips to keep in mind:

- **Lighting affects alertness and responsiveness.** Bright lights can be used to keep students alert, while dimmer lighting helps students calm down (Plitnick et al. 2010).

- **Different colors stimulate different parts of the brain.** Bright colors such as red and orange help stimulate students' creativity and excitement, while faded yellow and off-white help calm students down (Ravi Mehta 2009).

- **Different smells can be used for different purposes.** Peppermint and cinnamon make great scents for keeping students alert while lavender can be used to calm students.

- **Music can excite or calm students.** Classical and jazz pieces work great for free reading times, while hip hop and pop songs boost students' energy (Novotny 2013).

- **Texture can be used to calm students.** Create a texture book that includes swatches of different fabrics for students to feel as they read.

᪐ **Food and drink are powerful stimuli.** Allow students to eat and drink while they read. This creates a pleasurable experience associated with reading.

We know that the brain is wired for survival. The problem is that when the brain is in "survival mode," it cannot learn. Our challenge as educators is to create reading environments that tap into the curiosities of our students without creating the stress of the dreaded survival mode. We have used a number of multi-sensory tricks to help keep our students engaged and transition between different activities, including: allowing students to switch to seats in different parts of the room, changing where we stand to deliver instruction, wearing hats/special clothes, singing songs, providing students with healthy snacks and chances to rest, repeating/echoing exercises, conducting yoga/breathing activities, performing magic tricks, drawing, playing ball toss, changing tonality, and reading aloud interesting passages. The trick is variety, as all students have different ways of processing information.

Considering Multiple Intelligences

According to Harvard professor Howard Gardner (1991), students possess different kinds of minds and—therefore—learn, remember, perform, and understand in different ways. "We are all able to know the world through language, logical-mathematical analysis, spatial representation, musical thinking, the use of the body to solve problems or to make things, an understanding of other individuals, and an understanding of ourselves" (12). Gardner's Multiple Intelligences theory reveals that individuals differ in the strength of these intelligences and in the ways in which such intelligences are invoked and combined to carry out different tasks, solve diverse problems, and progress in various domains. (See Chapter 2 for descriptions of Gardner's Multiple Intelligences.)

Teachers need to constantly be aware of ways to attract their students' reading interests. We live in an age where multimedia options like television, video games, and the Internet pose significant competition to the written word. While watching television is a passive activity that requires little effort from the brain, reading is a much more interactive process that forces participants to think critically. Madeleine L'Engle (2015) observes:

In reading we must become creators. Once the child has learned to read alone, and can pick up a book without illustrations, he must become a creator, imagining the setting of the story, visualizing the characters, seeing facial expressions, hearing the inflection of voices. The author and the reader 'know' each other; they meet on the bridge of words.

So what can educators and parents do to make students more active participants in reading while addressing their multiple intelligences? Thomas Armstrong (2003) looks at literacy activities through Gardner's Multiple Intelligences and recommends some strategies. Figure 12.1 shows the types of intelligences, associated strategies, and suggested books.

Figure 12.1 Multiple Intelligences, Related Literacy Activities, and Sample Books

Type of Intelligence	Literacy Activities	Sample Books
Verbal-linguistic	Reading aloud	*Brown Bear, What Do You See?* by Bill Martin and Eric Carle *Alexander and the Terrible, Horrible, No Good, Very Bad Day* by Judith Viorst
Mathematical	Quantifying reading and writing processes	*Sir Cumference* series by Cindy Neuschwander and Wayne Geehan *The Grapes of Math* by Greg Tang *Actual Size* by Steve Jenkins
Bodily/ kinesthetic	Movement with reading and writing	*Klutz Book of Ridiculous Inventions* by John Cassidy and Brendan Boyle *Klutz Book of Paper Airplanes* by Doug Stillinger *We're Going on a Bear Hunt* by Helen Oxenbury and Michael Rosen
Spatial/visual	Visualizing and drawing	Pop-up books *Encyclopedia Prehistorica* series by Robert Sabuda and Matthew Reinhart *Wow! The Pop-up Book of Sports* by The Editors of Sports Illustrated Kids
Musical	Integrate music with reading and writing	Musical play books *The Backyardigans Musical Adventure* series by Publications International

Type of Intelligence	Literacy Activities	Sample Books
Interpersonal	Reading in pairs, groups, or whole class	Interactive books *Gallop! A Scanimation Book* by Rufus Butler Seder *Joyful Noise* by Paul Fleischman
Intrapersonal	Experiencing emotion	*The Adventures of Huckleberry Finn* by Mark Twain *First Day Jitters* by Julie Danneberg
Naturalist	Reading and writing in a natural setting	*The Tree in the Ancient Forest* by Carol Reed-Jones *Eliza and the Dragonfly* by Susie Caldwell Rinehart

The key for educators is to determine your objective and create different ways that different learners can demonstrate their understandings. When listening to a story, for example, teachers could ask verbal-linguistic learners to make a list of the key words being used, while mathematical learners could listen to the order or sequence of the story. Bodily kinesthetic learners could connect the story to physical actions, while visual spatial learners might want to concentrate to the words of the story and create pictures in their heads. Musical learners could listen to the sounds of the voices of the characters and author, interpersonal learners could pretend how listening changes for different people, and intrapersonal learners could concentrate on how a story makes them feel. Finally, naturalistic learners could relate the sounds they hear in a story to the sounds of nature.

We take the application of multiple intelligences a step further in Figure 12.2. This figure demonstrates cognitive associations people use when working on reading comprehension.

Figure 12.2 Cognitive Associations Involved in Reading Comprehension

Preferred Type of Intelligence	Favorite Reading Materials	Prompt
Verbal-Linguistic	Poetry Crosswords	Pay attention to the way the author puts words/phrases together. What vocabulary is included?
Mathematical	Mysteries Nonfiction	Identify a formula that summarizes this book.

Preferred Type of Intelligence	Favorite Reading Materials	Prompt
Bodily Kinesthetic	Action	What action can you do that will connect to the meaning of the book? Build artifacts to remind you of what you are reading.
Visual/Spatial	Descriptive texts with strong settings	Visualize the setting. Create a movie in your mind as you read. Design a new cover for the book.
Musical	Poetry Books with characters who have different voices	Listen to the rhythms of the characters' voice tones. Think about the audience hearing the voice of the author.
Interpersonal	Historical fiction Biographies	Identify with the character. Feel as if you are actually there.
Intrapersonal	Self-help Religion Philosophy	What questions are you asking? What happens when you agree with the author? Disagree?
Naturalistic	Nonfiction Natural settings	Identify the setting, the geography, the weather, the climate, and how that impacted the story.

Reading Makeover Quick Tips: Brain-Based Learning

Yvette Zgonc (2008) identifies several characteristics of a brain-based learning classroom that promotes reading. These activities are intended to build and maintain a positive culture in the classroom.

Social Interactions

- To establish relationships and connections, the teacher greets students at the door and asks them about what they are reading.

- To facilitate effective (invisible) discipline, the teacher uses many preventative strategies before interventions. For example, teaching the class Code of Conduct through multiple intelligences, providing opportunities for students to discharge energy, giving clear directions, offering lots of reading choices, being aware of students' emotional states and making changes when necessary.

- To plan interesting and motivating reading activities, the teacher uses class meetings. Class meetings are also used for problem solving.
- To concentrate on intrinsic reading motivation, the teacher celebrates accomplishments, provides for student choice, acknowledges efforts, and gives frequent feedback.

Classroom Environment

- To maintain a positive theme or positive affirmations, the teacher has posters and pictures around the room.
- To facilitate comfort and relaxation while reading, the teacher provides opportunities for students to sit in different places in the room.
- To maintain a calm and welcoming atmosphere, the teacher plays music before class, at the end of activities, during transitions between activities, during free reading time, and at other times as needed.

Instructional Practices

- To foster use of different memory pathways, the teacher includes field trips to access episodic memory, uses mnemonics to aid semantic memory, and fosters regular reading practice to build automaticity or procedural memory.
- To foster student reflection on learning, the teacher plans opportunities for downtime and helps students recognize that mistakes are opportunities for learning.
- To build student confidence, the teacher's lessons and activities involve challenging but non-threatening tasks.
- To enhance student independence, the teacher provides ongoing feedback about reading strategies.
- To accommodate different learning styles, the teacher is aware of multiple intelligences and provides frequent opportunities for enrichment in the auditory, kinesthetic, and visual realms.

David Sousa and Carol Ann Tomlinson (2010) examine a range of curricular, instructional, and assessment choices that factor into the extent to which students succeed in school. They observe:

"As we gain greater understanding of how the human brain works, we may discover ways to better meet the needs of our increasingly diverse student population. Sometimes students are attempting to learn in environments that are designed to help but inadvertently hinder their efforts" (5).

Conclusion

Understanding the physical and chemical factors of the brain can help us facilitate a learning environment that best meets our individual readers. Use Figure 12.1 to make a chart of your students that indicates what type of intelligence best matches their brain-based behavior and then find reading materials that relate. Go on a mission to take what you learned in this chapter and apply the "science of learning" to your pedagogy.

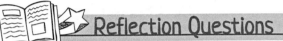 Reflection Questions

1. What are ways you can get parents to talk and listen more with their children at home?

2. How are boys' brains different than girls? What ways can you accommodate these differences to help struggling readers of either gender?

3. What things can you do in your classroom to make it a more multisensory environment?

4. Look at the cognitive associations in Figure 12.2. What materials would you select for a specific struggling reader with whom you work?

Chapter 13

Teamwork: The Thirteenth Step to Reading Riches

This chapter is not about you. It is about us. You cannot do a reading makeover alone. Together, we can accomplish great things. We discuss the importance of teamwork and how to build a team committed to building readers. We also offer some of the best practices we have seen in communicating as a team.

United Service Organizations (USO) promoters once asked entertainer Jimmy Durante to be a part of a show for World War II veterans (Hansel 2012). Durante told them that his schedule was very busy, and he could afford only a few minutes. He also assured the promoters that if they would not mind if he performed a short monologue so he could immediately leave for his next appointment, he would come. Of course, the show's promoters readily agreed. When Durante got on stage, however, something interesting happened. He went through his short monologue and then stayed. The applause grew louder and louder and he continued. Pretty soon, Durante had been on fifteen, twenty, then thirty minutes. Finally, he took a last bow and left the stage. Backstage, the promoters stopped him. "We thought you had to go after a few minutes," they said. "What happened?"

"I did have to go, but I can show you the reason I stayed," Durante replied. "You can see for yourself if you'll look down on the front row."

In the front row were two men, each of whom had lost an arm in the war. One had lost his right arm, and the other had lost his left. Together, they were able to clap, and that's exactly what they were doing, loudly and cheerfully.

It takes a village to produce a reader. The right teacher, administrator, or librarian can work wonders. Our best partners in assisting struggling and reluctant readers, however, are *parents*—hands down.

The Importance of Teamwork

Extraordinary teamwork leads to extraordinary accomplishments. Think of successful organizations that rely on teamwork to succeed: sports, military, medical, nonprofits, schools, businesses, politicians, countries. Even the most successful individuals have a team that contributes to their accomplishments. The late Steve Jobs, founder and CEO of Apple, once said, "We're great at figuring out how to divide things up into great teams that we have who all work on the same thing, touch base frequently, and bring it all together into a product" (Milian 2011, 1).

Effective Leaders

There is no mistaking it—effective leaders determine the success of every team. Strong leaders inspire their team and entire community to be involved and put forth their best effort. They model what it takes to succeed, motivate strong performers to keep striving for excellence, and inspire the weak to become strong (Kanold 2011). Leaders can be found throughout all levels of a school community: from the school board and superintendent, to teachers and student leaders in the classroom. Strong literacy programs have multiple leaders throughout their community—both in school and at home.

School principals should know and understand what their school needs to be successful in reading. Principals must find ways to make meaningful literacy connections between staff, parents, students, and the community. Classroom teachers should be current in research-based best practices surrounding literacy and implement those practices consistently in their classrooms.

Students can also play a significant leadership role in how they influence each other in various aspects of reading. Some students are natural leaders both inside the classroom and out, including some who may struggle with reading. These student leaders need guidance on the reading influence they can have on their peers. Adults need to acknowledge student leadership skills and help them use their talents in a way that can benefit those around them. At home, parents are the reading leaders. Parents should enforce a daily routine of reading and discussing books with their children.

McQueen (2015) recorded an interview with his former principal about all the things they encountered when they transformed their elementary school, notably about the role of leadership, in their reading makeover. They discuss important things to consider when making decisions: how low-performing schools can't have leaders making decisions in a "vacuum" and in some cases, power must actually be taken away from people who previously held it. Visit www. ProfessionalDevelopmentForTeachers. com/Escaped-Disaster Leadership to learn about the process and decisions involved in implementing a reading makeover in the school.

Collaboration

There is nothing better in education than a group of dedicated teachers, parents, and support staff working collaboratively to improve the literacy lives of students. Greg Anrig (2015) reviews evidence for collaboration and notes that "success stories are emerging that begin with administrators reaching out to teachers and their unions to develop a more inclusive culture focused on improving the learning experience of all students" (30). *Relational trust* among administrators, teachers, and parents is an essential element in successful collaborative efforts. Some of the most compelling evidence for such success is the research from the University of Chicago's Consortium on Chicago School Research (Bryk et al. 2010).

Anrig (2015) identifies five organizational features that contributed to this success.

1. A coherent instructional guidance system, in which curriculum and assessment were coordinated within and across grades with meaningful teacher involvement.

2. An effective system to improve professional capacity by providing ongoing support and guidance for teachers.

3. Strong ties among school personnel, parents, and community service providers, with an integrated support network for students.

4. A student-centered learning climate that identified and responded to problems individual students were experiencing.

5. Leadership focused on cultivating teachers, parents, and community members so that they became invested in sharing responsibility for the school's improvement (31).

Diverse backgrounds, experiences, and insights of the collective group help ensure that struggling readers receive the extra support they need. Strong schools teach collaboration techniques and practice these on a daily basis. Literacy collaborating can look different, depending on the need and which team members are involved. Working together, the school staff can create a culture that serves all students. This means maintaining a focus on what matters, addressing organizational challenges, and learning from data (Chenoworth 2015). Student contributions must be provided for with the necessary support and respectful follow-up. Eric Hardie (2015) maintains that, "all schools have the resources required—they just need to start *really* listening to their students" (94). Finally, parent involvement is necessary if students, notably those who struggle with learning, are to achieve success (Henderson et al. 2011). Effective collaboration in schools involves staff, students, and parents.

Communication

Good communication can help teams accomplish their goals more quickly. As in any relationship, asking clarifying questions, sharing concerns, and discussing ideas can proactively prevent many problems, especially when struggling readers are involved. For example, when teachers and parents discuss reading concerns right away, both parties feel valued and encouraged to find a solution together, instead of feeling they have to trudge through it alone. When staff members are teaming up to discuss a student's reading problems, it's important to listen to each other and engage all members of the team to be active listeners. Strong team leaders ensure effective communication happens throughout the entire team.

When a member of the team takes a risk to share something, they must feel that their thoughts and opinions will be valued and respected by whomever is listening. The more often this happens, the more likely they will want to open up again in the future. This form of trust leads to stronger relationships, better communication, and a more effective team.

Communicating effectively also involves using the right tools at the right time. In some cases sending an email is a perfect way to get clarification, discuss minor situations, or even share a few concerns. However, more serious conversations that involve sensitive topics or emotional situations will likely warrant a phone call or even a face-to-face conversation. It is far too easy to blast off an email to avoid a long, difficult conversation, but just like we teach our students—engaging in more personal communication is better, especially when dealing with a challenge.

Finally, struggling readers should be an integral part of the ongoing communication process, especially students who may be shy, frustrated, intimidated, or even afraid for one reason or another. Talk with them often in an honest and respectful manner. Make sure you get them to talk and share what issues they are feeling and experiencing. When you are an active listener and show them you care, you will gain their trust and get them to open up. This is when true learning becomes possible.

Relationships

When you organize a diverse group of staff, parents, and students to be part of a school's reading makeover team, creating strong relationships will make your team more effective. The closer you become with each other, both personally and professionally, the more you will trust each other, open up, and take risks to solve problems. Informal get-togethers, team-building activities, and relationship exercises help create a strong team. "Knowing each other's stories not only helps us to work together well, but also builds trust and encourages us to further develop our intergroup skills" (Chapman 2014, 36).

The more often you support each other in addressing the problems of your struggling readers, the stronger your relationships will become. Your close, caring support for each other will intrinsically motivate each other and let you hold each other accountable for various tasks and responsibilities. Great teamwork takes sacrifice and a willingness to be unselfish. As you grow and learn together to address the needs of your readers, you will have a much better chance of achieving your goals, both individually and school wide.

Truths and Benefits of Parent Involvement

Educational consultant Yvette Zgonc (2008) insists that parents are central contributors to students' success, especially struggling and reluctant readers. All parents have hopes and dreams for their children, and it is critical that educators recognize that parents are doing the best they can with what they have. Successful parent involvement nurtures relationships between parents and children and partnerships between educators and parents.

Struggling and reluctant readers' success and achievement in reading are enhanced when parents play active roles in their children's reading progress. When educators nurture relationships with parents, parents develop a more positive attitude toward school, children, and themselves. Research suggests that, in turn, parents become more involved in their communities and develop deeper beliefs about the importance of their children's education (Henderson and Mapp 2002). The most successful educators go to great lengths to ensure that the parents of their struggling and reluctant readers recognize their importance in their children's reading progress. Everybody wants to feel important.

Legendary college football coach Paul "Bear" Bryant once offered his views on putting together a successful, winning team. As a coach, he understood how to lift some people up and how to calm down others, until finally they functioned as a successful unit. "If anything goes bad, I did it," he said. "If anything goes semi-good, then we did it. If anything goes real good, then you did it" (Bryant 2012, 1).

LESSONS LEARNED FROM MIKE & DANNY

Danny: My success with my students can be directly attributed to the participation of their parents. Period. Parents always played a huge factor in the greatest miracles I witnessed with struggling and reluctant readers.

I used to point out to parents that they had the greatest "home field advantage" in history. "You might be the worst parent on the planet," I said. "But your kid doesn't know it. To your child, you are simply Mom or Dad." Children idolize their parents, even the ones who make tons of mistakes. Parents are our most significant teachers, and they need to hear how important they are.

It is important for people to understand the numbers 24/7/365/8,760: there are 24 hours in a day, 7 days a week, 365 days a year totaling 8,760 hours in a year. People need to also remember the numbers 6/5/180/1,080: there are typically 6 hours in a school day, 5 days a week, 180 days a year equaling 1,080 hours in a typical school year. Do the math, and subtract 1,080 from 8,760. You should get the number 7,680. There are 7,680 hours each year that students are with parents, rather than teachers. That means that no matter what I do as a child's teacher, his parents are nearly seven times more important than me.

Mike: The score was tied with only 10 seconds left in double overtime, and I had the basketball. My team, Concordia University Wisconsin, had the chance to do the unthinkable: beat the University of Wisconsin Parkside for the first time in school history. Now, we were not competing against just any ordinary team. We were battling the same head coach who had cut me from his team exactly one year earlier, only now I was on the opposing squad hoping to show him what a mistake he made. My teammates knew the disappointment and heartache I went through after getting cut and how badly I wanted to prove the coach wrong. As we left the locker room to start the game, my coach inspired the whole team by saying, "Let's win this one for McQueen!"

To my disappointment, I didn't play well the entire game. I tried my best but couldn't make a shot to save my life. Despite my frustrating performance, my teammates picked up the slack. They dove to the floor to grab loose balls, ran as fast as they could the entire game, and gave me encouragement and hope to stay positive. In the performance of his career, my teammate, Joe Toniazzo, came off the bench and scored a personal record 35 points to keep us in the game and give us a chance at the end to pull off a miracle victory.

So there I was, dribbling toward the hoop with 10 seconds left. My other teammate, Frank Yinko, flashed to the middle, I passed him the ball, and he made a last second shot to win the game!

Reflecting back at our victory, there were many components that made us an amazing team. We had to quickly diagnose different problems that came up and then rely on each other to figure out the best solutions, including key players that stepped up to accept extraordinary challenges. We had to talk to each other throughout the entire game. We had to point out each other's mistakes and encourage each other to improve, and then keep fighting until the very end.

We know that the reading challenges in many schools can be daunting and sometimes feel impossible to overcome. Have faith that your team can pull off a last-second victory. Recruit strong leaders, and create a school-wide vision that inspires everyone. Define clear, reachable goals, and build strong relationships throughout your team. Collaborate, communicate, and fight until the very end. Remember, you never know what great things can happen unless you work as a team and give it your best shot.

Reading Makeover Quick Tips: Collaborating

As described earlier in this chapter, successful schools build on the collaborative efforts of the staff, students, and parents. Here are some reminders of activities that support cooperative efforts.

Staff

- **Co-Plan.** Reach out to your teacher-librarian, instructional coach, administrator, reading specialist, and anyone else that can help you tackle whatever reading problems need to be addressed to get your struggling readers motivated, focused, and on the path of improvement.

- **Team-Teach.** When more than one staff member joins forces to teach a unit, it allows students to gain exposure to learning from a wider variety of experiences, perspectives, and styles.

- **Keep Administrators Involved.** Reach out to your principal, assistant principal, school board members, or any other staff members. Ask them to read a book, get involved with a reading event or program teach, or maybe mentor a struggling reader.

- ❧ **Collaborate Horizontally.** Work closely with teachers in the same grade level or content area.

- ❧ **Collaborate Vertically.** Work closely with teachers who educate students at different age levels.

- ❧ **Join Forces.** Connect with other schools in your area that are facing similar reading challenges. Addressing the needs of struggling readers varies from school to school and it's usually very beneficial to share ideas, support, and resources.

Students

- ❧ **Encourage students to participate in leadership opportunities**, both inside and outside of school. There are many opportunities such as student council, scouts, reader's theater, sports, camps, and more!

- ❧ **Help students observe what happens when people work together.** Encourage them to learn from their teachers and classmates.

- ❧ **Encourage students to assist classmates** when they need help with tasks that they do well and enjoy.

- ❧ **Provide opportunities for students to read to younger students.** This can be done at school or at home.

- ❧ **Encourage students to take advantage of programs for readers at the local library.** A schedule of events can often be found on the library website.

- ❧ **Provide opportunities for students to volunteer.** This can be done at community or school events where extra help is needed.

Parents

- **Remind parents that they are their child's best teacher.** The example they set will be what their child initially follows.

- **Encourage parents to take advantage of frequent opportunities to read with their kids and talk with them about what they're reading.** This can be done by reading aloud to them, reading in front of them, letting their children see them enjoying reading, and taking them to the library or bookstores.

- **Remind parents that they can model reading behavior.** This can be done when they are looking at grocery store flyers, cutting out coupons, reading sports scores, and more.

- **Encourage parents to help their children choose reading materials and support them in the choices they make.** This can be done by going to the local library or used bookstore to find materials that interest their children.

- **Let parents know about Internet resources that encourage reading and writing.** For example, www.sixwordmemoirs.com/teens is a site that invites kids to write stories that are only six words long

- **Remind parents that you welcome them to meet with you.** They can meet about school activities and lessons or even social and emotional concerns, as well.

- **Encourage parents to participate in parent-teacher-school activities.** This allows them to provide input to discussions and understand that they have a venue to advocate for their children and learn about what's going on at school.

Conclusion

Teamwork is an essential component to a successful reading makeover, whether the makeover is contained in one classroom or expanded throughout the entire school. Finding great leaders and setting them up for success is foundational to positive change. Create strong relationships and help them thrive through good communication and effective collaboration. As you work together, you will be much more effective and be able to reach your reading goals. Involve a wide range of team members and inspire them to share your passion.

 Reflection Questions

1. Describe a team that has been successful in the real world (sports, business, family). Who were they? What made them successful?

2. What characteristics should we look for in a strong reading leader?

3. What barriers can get in the way of good communication? How do we overcome those barriers?

4. Why is collaboration important? What are different ways that your students, teachers, and parents can collaborate with reading?

Chapter 14

The Secrets: The Final Steps to Reading Riches

We all know that reading is important, but what should we keep at the forefront of our thoughts and actions as we work with students? How do we get our students fired-up about reading, especially the ones who have difficulty or poor attitudes? How do we get them to experience the beauty, power, and importance of something that they do not understand or view as unnecessary? What is the secret? Throughout this book, we have touched on many different components that shed light on what we know works to inspire students, especially struggling readers. This chapter consolidates the most important concepts and sets the tone for the last chapter.

One day a traveler was walking along a road on his journey from one village to another. As he walked he noticed a monk tending the ground in the fields beside the road. The monk said, "Good day" to the traveler, and the traveler nodded to the monk. The traveler then turned to the monk and said, "Excuse me, do you mind if I ask you a question?"

"Not at all," replied the monk.

"I am traveling from the village in the mountains to the village in the valley, and I was wondering if you knew what it is like in the village in the valley?"

"Tell me," said the monk, "What was your experience of the village in the mountains?"

"Dreadful," replied the traveler. "To be honest I am glad to be away from there. I found the people most unwelcoming. When I first arrived I was greeted coldly. I was never made to feel part of the village no matter how hard I tried. The villagers keep very much to themselves; they don't take kindly to strangers. So tell me, what can I expect in the village in the valley?"

"I am sorry to tell you," said the monk, "but I think your experience will be much the same there."

The traveler hung his head despondently and walked on. A while later, another traveler was journeying down the same road, and he also came upon the monk.

"I'm going to the village in the valley," said the second traveler. "Do you know what it is like?"

"I do," replied the monk. "But first, tell me—where have you come from?"

"I've come from the village in the mountains."

"And how was that?"

"It was a wonderful experience. I would have stayed if I could, but I am committed to traveling on. I felt as though I was a member of the family in the village. The elders gave me much advice, the children laughed and joked with me, and people were generally kind and generous. I am sad to have left there. It will always hold special memories for me. And what of the village in the valley?" he asked again.

"I think you will find it much the same," replied the monk. "Good day to you."

"Good day, and thank you," the traveler replied, smiled, and journeyed on.

Mindset is everything. But it is not just a positive attitude. A positive attitude cannot make a child a reader. It can, however, help a struggling or reluctant reader infinitely more than a negative attitude. Teachers, administrators, and parents can truly make students readers by passing along a love of reading built around access to wonderful reading materials, time to read, and read alouds. Our mission is to help students see themselves as good readers and we have used plenty of tricks from our teaching arsenal to achieve this, including:

- campfires
- traditions
- attitudes
- love

Campfires

Campfires are awesome. A good campfire appeals to our senses: it keeps us warm, melts our delicious marshmallows, attracts our attention with pops and crackles, hypnotizes us with dancing flames, and fills the air with a wonderful smell. Campfires are great to enjoy when we are alone and even better when we are with people we care about. They serve as a beacon of entertainment, allowing us to share stories, engage in meaningful conversations, and create lifelong memories that will strengthen our relationships with those we care about. It only takes one great campfire experience to get us hooked.

Unfortunately, some people are not able to appreciate a good campfire. Gathering the materials and building the fire can be filthy, frustrating work—especially when the weather is not cooperating. The smell of smoke can be irritating to some, and the dangers of fire can be frightening—especially for those who have been burned. Many people have never even seen or experienced a campfire, so they do not know what they are missing.

For many students, reading is a lot like the mysteries of a campfire. They know it is important and see many other people enjoying it, but it is a secret that they just cannot quite figure out. For other students, reading is even worse; it is like the campfire that they could not start or the one that burned them.

Traditions

Traditions are a huge part of every culture. As parents and teachers, we develop routines and patterns so that our students can experience great things and hopefully share these experiences one day with their own children. Think about all the things that we pass down to future generations:

- **Skills:** cooking, playing instruments, fixing cars
- **Love:** hugs; words; gifts; compliments; needs like food, shelter, and clothing
- **Media:** movies, TV shows, music
- **Traditions:** holidays, vacations, Sunday dinners
- **Faith:** church, scripture, rites, hymns
- **Opinions:** politics, stereotypes
- **Bad habits:** driving behaviors, biting nails, bad language

Since we do not teach parenting in school, most of us just do the same things that our parents did with us. If our parents read every night at bedtime, we probably do that with our kids. But what if reading is not a part of a family's daily life? What if their home is not filled with books, magazines, comics, and other reading materials? What if nobody ever talks about reading at home? Sadly enough, this situation is common for many struggling readers, especially during the first five years of their lives. Educators must find out what a student's reading home environment life is like. If we discover parents who lack skill, desire, or confidence in reading, then we should consider intervening by inspiring and educating them (Henderson et al. 2011). Once reading routines are established at home, the benefits carry over with students into the classroom and throughout their lives.

And what about traditions in schools that may not be the best for students? In Mike's first year as a teacher-librarian, he followed the same rule that the librarian before him used: students could not check out nonfiction books until they were in third grade. How horrible is that? Changing that rule was not as easy as you would think. Primary teachers feared these books were counterproductive for their students learning to read. They felt the books were way too difficult to read. They mistakenly thought these books consumed too much time and energy compared to checking out books that students could read. Mike managed to change the rule in his second year, and kids were allowed to check out multiple books, including any book of their choice—fiction or nonfiction. Just like at home, our school environment needs reading traditions that are best for our students.

Attitudes

As we discussed in Chapter 9, there are two types of motivation: *extrinsic motivation,* in which outside factors influence one's desire to perform a task, and *intrinsic motivation,* in which one performs a task out of an internal desire rather than for an outside reward. Believe us: we have seen external motivation work to encourage reading, but too often—in our view—external rewards send the message to students that reading is not a reward in itself. Students are smart; they know if you have to bribe them to do something, it probably is not worth doing. We believe that true motivation comes from within ourselves.

Intrinsically motivating our students to have determination and positive attitudes toward reading is much more important than focusing too much on their reading levels or test performance results. Instilling a love and passion toward reading will help their skills and ability to improve naturally. If you give students daily opportunities to read for fun in a nonpressured atmosphere, students will have a much better attitude toward reading. The more they like to read, the more likely they are to read. The more they read, the stronger readers they will become.

Struggling readers need to learn about *grit*, and the important role that it plays in getting them through the reading challenges they face. They need to know that struggling at something is an important part of the process. Grit is more than determination, it is a "firmness of mind or spirit: unyielding courage in the face of hardship or danger" (Merriam Webster). Learning to read takes grit. Angela Lee Duckworth (2013) says that when kids read and learn about the brain and how it grows when it is challenged, they are much more likely to persevere when they fail because they do not believe that failure is a permanent position. So when our readers struggle, let's discuss grit and explain the importance of failure and how overcoming it builds our character. When we ask audiences what the opposite of success is, the majority of people say that the opposite of success is failure. We totally disagree. In order to succeed at

anything—reading included—you have to fail again and again. No, the opposite of success is not trying or giving up.

As adults, it is important to have a good attitude at our jobs. There is no doubt that being an educator is tough work, especially during tough financial times, political unrest, and test pressure. When we have the right mindset to look beyond the surface and focus our attitudes on what is important, the joy and passion we hold in our hearts can defeat any anger or negativity and make our environments more positive, which will inspire our students to learn. When we get down on ourselves and morale is low, authors Megan and Bob Tschannen-Moran (2014) emphasize the importance of focusing on strengths. We do amazing work as teachers. Let's be proud, and let our positive attitudes shine brightly and rub off on our students.

We need to have faith that our efforts make a difference in the lives of those around us, especially in our students. In our mission to help our students, we all stumble and fall sometimes—we are only human. We must believe that we are not alone and remember that we are all in this together. When this happens, get help from your team, get back on your feet, and dust yourself off. We do not often see the fruits of our labor. We give, give, give, until one day, poof—the students are off to the next phase of their lives and gone from ours. Hopefully, we have a positive impact in our limited time with our students.

LESSONS LEARNED FROM MIKE & DANNY

Mike: One of my biggest goals as a parent has always been to maintain strong relationships—founded on faith and love—with both of my daughters. My heart smiles when I think back to the numerous daddy-daughter dates I have been on with my girls. Thanks to my wonderful wife, Jeanne, I started going on daddy-daughter dates with our girls when they were toddlers and continued them through their entire childhoods (even now, during college). One tradition that we started involved visiting a library or bookstore. We would get books and chill out with ice cream while we talked and leisurely looked through our treasures.

With almost every visit to the bookstore or library, I made a point to do the following things:

- model how to ask a staff member to help me find a book, magazine, or comic book

- browse through the material as a preview before deciding to keep it
- show my excitement afterwards
- ask my daughters to tell me about what they chose and what they liked about their books.

Once in a while, all three of us would go on a "double-daddy-daughter-date." My favorite parts of these dates were watching both daughters share and talk with each other after they found their books. The impact they had on each other was just as meaningful, if not more, than my influence on them.

By modeling these behaviors over and over and over again, my girls knew how important reading was. Our reading-based daddy-daughter dates strengthened our love for each other, as well as our love for literacy. Instilling this love of reading into their hearts has been one of the greatest gifts that I could have ever given them. There is no doubt that our reading traditions will continue the day I am a grandparent.

Danny: Reading determines everything. Charley "Tremendous" Jones, a motivational leader whose goal was to help people empower their lives through reading, said "you will be the same person in five years as you are today except for the people you meet and the books you read" (Jones 2015).

When I was a teacher, I taught in an inner-city school district where plenty of negative people and influences surrounded my students. Books offered them not only answers to their questions, but also provided positive role models to show my students how people just like them had turned negative circumstances into highly successful careers in business, government, sports, entertainment, philanthropy— you name it.

Have you ever heard the expression "readers are leaders"? I am not convinced of that. I have met a fair share of folks who read plenty and never get around to applying anything that they read. It reminds me of something I often used to hear when I taught: good readers are good writers. That was not always the case.

No, one of the joys I have learned on my lifetime journey is that some of the best thoughts come from standing conventional wisdom on its head. So, instead of "business before pleasure," I often choose "pleasure before business." Rather than eating dinner before dessert, some situations call for enjoying dessert before dinner. I have met plenty of good readers who are not necessarily good writers, but I have never met a good writer who is not an avid reader.

The same is true for leadership. I have met plenty of readers who may not necessarily be leaders, but I have never met a leader who does not devour a healthy diet of books, magazines, newspapers, and other reading materials. Translation: Leaders = Readers.

It is imperative to me that students understand that the power to succeed lies within them, largely based on the choices they make. If you have any desire to be a leader, know that you must be a reader. Also realize, though, that reading is not enough. I used to always tell my students that education is valuable, but execution is priceless.

Want to know the "secret" to creating a successful reading makeover? Here it is: it is not one thing, but lots of little things. It is the daily habits we instill in our students: providing them plenty of different engaging reading materials to choose from, giving them time to read in class, reading aloud to them—all the things we have been talking about. W. Clement Stone said, "Big doors swing on little hinges" (Stone 2015, 1). Implement the tips we provide in this book. Start small, and think big. You might not be able to do everything we suggest, but please, do something.

Love

How do we transfer our love of reading to students and inspire them to gather around the "reading campfire?" It may sound obvious, but it all starts with love. John Lennon was right when he wrote the song, *All You Need is Love*. Whether our students realize it or not, they crave love, especially students who lack love at home or in school. Students need to feel our care and concern on a daily basis. The better we get to know them (their hobbies, aspirations, problems and anything else we can discover), the better we can connect with them and help them with their needs. Conversely, when we let students into our world and help them get to know us, we build trust and appreciation—leading to mutual respect. Respect leads to a loving relationship, and relationships are the foundation to a love of literacy.

Modeling your love of reading cannot be overemphasized. It is one thing to tell students to read, and it is another thing entirely to show them. The more students see different people reading (both adults and peers), the more likely it will influence them to read. Witnessing readers is not enough, though: students need to consistently engage in conversations and activities that remind them why reading is helpful, important, and needed.

As teachers, we cannot just "talk the talk;" we have to "walk the walk." Students need to see our love of reading by our actions. Read aloud to students using energy and passion. Take them to the library or bookstore and engage them in conversations about their reading interests and yours, as well. Show them how to approach a librarian or bookseller and ask for assistance in finding a title. Once you find the book or magazine, let them see how you preview it and talk about something that excites you (be creative if needed).

Talking about reading inspires a love of reading. Help students connect reading to their experiences and interests. Ask them questions about what books they are reading, how they found them, how they like them, what their books are about and why they chose to read those particular books. It is also very powerful to talk about other authors and books that relate to materials they are reading. Bridging their text to other materials helps "stoke their fires" and feed their reading hunger.

It is critical to be a good listener, too. Your body language and nonverbal skills make a difference when students speak about reading. Focus 100 percent of your attention on the students you are talking with, and avoid distractions like cellphones, interruptions, and other things that may be on your mind. The better listener you are, the more compassion you will exude to the students you are working with.

Share your own stories that relate to materials that you love to read. In Danny's studies of students' reading habits, he has found that books introduced by teachers are among the most popular titles read by students. Every time Mike tells students about his love of the *Guinness Book of World Records*, the books fly off the library shelves no matter what age the students are. Reading-related stories work best if you pick examples that connect with the students' interests, but even just modeling excitement for your own materials sends the right message. Tap into the power of peer conversations, too. Students take advice and reading recommendations from one another much more often than simply listening to adults. Teachers should set up guidelines and procedures to implement peer-reading discussions. Parents can also promote these discussions by shuttling children and their friends on frequent visits to the library or bookstore and let them engage in conversations afterwards.

Finally, do not let test pressure ruin the love of reading. Our mission is to infect students with a lifelong love of learning that books make possible. Make

sure to schedule at least 15–20 minutes each day for self-selected independent reading time. Luring students to read materials they would not normally choose is a very delicate, risky task, especially as students get older. It can be done (especially the more students love you), but forcing topics or materials can quickly turn a love of reading into hatred. Provide students with plenty of choices, remembering that there are literally hundreds of thousands of titles produced in English every year. You are bound to find something students enjoy!

Reading Makeover Quick Tips: Share the Secrets

- **Be Brave:** The more struggling readers you have, the harder and scarier it can seem. No matter how big the obstacles are, stay strong and don't lose faith.

- **Be Determined:** If there's a will, there's a way! Set SMART goals, have a sense of urgency to complete them, and then truly believe that both you and your students can succeed!

- **Teach About Grit:** Model how you overcome your own struggles with difficult text. Show students how you used grit to make it through and let them all share their examples, too.

- **Stay Positive:** Don't let hardships bring you down, no matter what they are. When fussy students or parents try to darken your attitude, turn on the light and smother them with positivity. A good attitude is essential.

- **Don't Make Excuses:** Be respectful and empathetic for the personal problems that many struggling readers bring with them to school, but don't let struggling readers use those excuses as a way to get out of work. The same goes for us.

- **Model Reading:** Constantly show why reading is important and how it improves your life. Then, connect your students with other people that can do the same.

- **Bond with the "Naughty" Ones:** There are good reasons why students misbehave, so be patient and persistent. Everyone has gifts and talents waiting to be unleashed. Strong relationships are the foundation to learning.

- **Show Love:** Your struggling readers will climb mountains when they feel your love and know that their academic success is important to you.

Conclusion

The positive reading experiences and traditions that we plant with students now are the seeds that will be with them forever. Inspire your students to nurture their seeds and to grow them with a positive attitude, passion, and love.

Reflection Questions

1. Think of something that a friend or loved one convinced you to do that was outside of your comfort zone. How did they inspire you to do it? How can you transfer that experience to help your struggling readers?

2. Describe a reading tradition that you have experienced in the past. How can you use this experience to help struggling readers you work with?

3. What factors can cause struggling readers to have a bad attitude? What can we do to help address those factors?

4. Why is it so important to model a love of reading, especially to our struggling readers? What specific things can we do to model this love?

Your Challenge

You've made it to the most important part of the book: our challenge to you. We hope this chapter will help you examine your learning environment and practices as a professional, and motivate you to make any changes that will benefit your students. We hope to inspire you to take action!

When motivational speaker and writer Denis Waitley (Newhouse 1998) was just a young boy, his father abandoned his family. That left nine-year-old Denis as the oldest boy in the house.

There was an army emplacement near his home during World War II. In order to befriend the children in the area, the soldiers would give them little canteens, army helmets, and gun belts. In return, the children would do favors for the soldiers. They would run their errands, bring them candy, get them home cooking—just about anything.

One day a soldier said to Denis, "I want to take you fishing in a boat." Denis had never been fishing out in the ocean; he had always fished off a bridge. He was so excited that he sneaked out of his bedroom window, got his tackle box, packed himself a lunch and put it in the refrigerator. At 4 a.m. he was ready to go with his fishing pole, tackle box, and lunch. There he was sitting on the curb, waiting.

The soldier never came.

Denis says that probably was the turning point of his life. Instead of being either cynical or telling his Mom and his friends that the soldier never came, he got himself a one-man rubber life raft. After inflating it, he went down to the bay and pretended that he was launching this marvelous fishing boat. Then he went out in the bay where he dug some clams, caught fish, and had what he called the most marvelous day of his life. That experience taught Denis an important lesson: we can't rely on others to make our dreams come true. If our dreams are to be realized, we must step out on faith and accomplish them ourselves.

What does it ultimately take to turn a struggling and/or reluctant reader into a passionate reader?

LESSONS LEARNED FROM MIKE & DANNY

Mike: There are two things that I am deathly afraid of: lightning and dancing in public. I can easily avoid dancing, but lightning is not always in my control.

For more than 10 years I taught a week-long "Mountain Search and Rescue" class during the summer to 25 middle-school students. One year we were on a training mission three miles from base camp, off trail, and we had just made it to the top of a steep plateau when a student said, "Mr. McQueen, look at those clouds in the distance." When I saw that these dark demons were heading our way, the hair on the back of my neck stood up (figuratively speaking), and I calmly shouted to the group, "We need to head back down, now!"

Despite a lot of bickering and moaning, we quickly scuttled back down the steep climb, and just as we made it to tree line, the loudest crack of thunder that I have ever heard pierced our ears. I gathered everyone together, and we cowered under a plastic tarp as a torrential downpour of rain and lightning pounded us for five straight horrifying minutes. This time, the hairs on my arms were literally standing up. During this terrifying ordeal, I estimate that more than 50 bolts of lightning struck, all within a few hundred yards of us. Despite my fear, I stayed calm, hid my terror, and by the good grace of God, we avoided a potentially tragic situation.

After the storm passed, we were soaking wet, cold, and emotionally distraught, with one student crying uncontrollably. Knowing we still had a long three-mile slippery descent ahead of us, I collected my wits, calmed the hysterical student, organized us into small groups, and discussed a plan that required teamwork if we wanted to make it back safely. The next few hours proved to be extremely difficult as we slipped and scrambled, arm-in-arm, back down the mountain. It took a lot of focus, grit, and teamwork, but we did it. We made it to base camp uninjured. Although we were exhausted, both physically and emotionally, we had a story that we would remember for the rest of our lives.

Helping struggling readers can be just as scary, frustrating, and difficult as our experience on the mountain. We made it through because someone pointed out the warning signs, I faced my fears, and we worked together to accomplish our mission. Keep your eyes open for the warning signs in your classroom, home, or school: bad reading attitudes, low morale in class or school, uninvolved parents or educators. Think of this story (and this entire book) to help you succeed with a reading makeover. Everyone can make a difference: teachers, parents, librarians, administrators, teacher-assistants, custodians, and office staff. Accomplishing our goal took careful planning, a lot of determination, hard work, and a dedicated team. How will you handle your storm?

Danny: Two stories come to mind, one involving a college professor, the other a bottle of perfume (no, this is not a joke).

A college professor prepared a test for his soon-to-be-graduating seniors. The test questions were divided into three categories and the students were instructed to choose questions from only one of the categories. The first category of questions was the hardest and worth fifty points. The second, which was easier, was worth forty points. The third, the simplest, was worth thirty points. Upon completion of the test, students who had chosen the hardest fifty-point questions were given A's. The students who had chosen the forty-point questions received B's. Those who settled for the easiest thirty-pointers were given C's. The students were frustrated with the grading of their papers and asked the professor what he was looking for.

"I wasn't testing your knowledge," the professor explained, as he leaned over the podium with a bright grin. "I was testing your goals."

Katherine Elliot (cited in Clarke 1998, January 25) writes that when she was about 10 years old, her grandmother received a gift of perfume in a bottle that fascinated young Katherine. Made of green pottery with a long, slender neck and a square bottom, it looked like pictures Katherine has seen of ancient ware. She begged her grandmother to open it.

"No," Grandma always said. "I'm going to save it until later."

When Katherine was 33, her grandmother gave her the perfume saying, "Let's see how long you can keep it without opening it."

One day, many years later, Katherine picked up the perfume bottle. She was shocked to discover that it was empty, although still sealed. Turning it over, she could see why. The bottom of the bottle had never been glazed. The perfume had slowly evaporated through the porous clay. How sad that no one ever enjoyed the perfume—not Katherine, nor her grandmother, or anyone else! How disappointing that no one had ever utilized such a precious gift.

Why do we share these three stories? Well, they seem to encompass the gist of what a reading makeover truly entails.

It is imperative that you set high goals for your students. To paraphrase Michelangelo, "The greater challenge is not that we set our goals too high and miss them, but that we set them too low and reach them." Every student is capable of accomplishing whatever he or she believes. Sometimes, we need someone else to believe in us before we believe in ourselves. The more we see out students as readers, the more they will see themselves as readers.

Next, it is important to realize that nothing we have described in this book is easy. Some of the ideas we offer may be simple, but none are easy. It takes time to create passionate readers. We wish it was as easy as downloading a reading program into every student's mind the same way Keanu Reeves quickly learns his sophisticated fighting skills in *The Matrix*, but—then again—we have found that the only things truly worth having take time, patience and, in many cases, a lot of blood, sweat, and tears.

Finally, it is important that none of us take for granted the many gifts we possess. Like Katherine Elliot's bottle of perfume, how often do we fail to use our gifts because of shyness, selfishness, or just plain laziness?

Want your students to be readers? People can blame poor schools, negligent parents, limited resources, learning disabilities—whatever. The fact remains that it is important that we step out on faith and do whatever it takes to make reading a reality for our struggling and reluctant readers. Don't wait for your ship to come in; swim out to it. There are some people who spend their lives waiting for a break, an opportunity—a winning lottery ticket. That is not how life works. That is not how reading works. Becoming a lifelong reader is a journey, and it is our hope that you accept this mission, this challenge, this honor, with pride, enthusiasm, and joy.

Conclusion

Have you been battling poor reading attitudes, low morale, or inadequate reading performance? Do you worry that the love of reading is dwindling away from your students or that your parents or teachers just don't understand the things we discussed in this book? Have politics and standardized test pressure lured you into boring reading routines that are turning students off to reading? If you answered "yes" to any of these questions, then there is no doubt—*now* is the time to make a change and accept our challenge to do a reading makeover. Go for it! If needed, start small and test our advice on a few specific struggling readers, or step it up a notch and focus on an entire class. If your school is overdue for a big change, do a book study with this book, get the parents involved, and assemble a school-wide team to create a plan. Whatever you do, just don't wait to get started. Take action right now and start brainstorming steps that you can start tomorrow. Stand up for the readers you care about and put your thoughts into action.

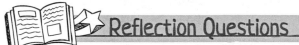

Reflection Questions

1. Identify three struggling readers who can serve as an anonymous inspiration for you to do a reading makeover.

2. What obstacles might hold you back from doing a reading makeover?

3. Who can you team-up with to start your reading makeover?

4. What are the first steps you need to take?

References Cited

Alexander, Patricia A., and Tamara L. Jetton. 2000. "Learning from Text: A Multidimensional and Developmental Perspective." In *Handbook of Reading Research*, edited by Michael L. Kamil, Peter B. Mosenthal, P. David Pearson, and Rebecca Barr (3): 285–310. Mahwah, NJ: Erlbaum.

Allen, George. 1989. *Strategies for Winning: A Top Coach's Game Plan for Victory in Football and in Life.* New York, NY: McGraw-Hill.

Allen, Patrick A. 2009. *Conferring: the Keystone of Reader's Workshop.* Portland, ME: Stenhouse Publishers.

Allen, Patrick, Lori L. Conrad, Missy Matthews, and Cheryl Zimmerman. 2008. *Put Thinking to the Test.* Portland, ME: Stenhouse Publishers.

Allington, Richard L. 2011. "What At-Risk Readers Need." *Educational Leadership*, 68(6): 40-45 http://www.ascd.org/publications/educational_leadership/mar11/vol68/num06/What_At-Risk_Readers_Need.aspx.

Allington, Richard L., and Sean Walmsley, eds. 1995. *No Quick Fix: Rethinking Literacy Programs in America's Elementary Schools.* New York, NY: Teachers College Press.

Allington, Richard, and Patricia Cunningham. 2007. *Schools That Work: Where All Children Read and Write.* New York, NY: Pearson.

Anrig, Greg. 2015. "How We Know Collaboration Works." *Educational Leadership*, 72(8): 30-35 http://www.ascd.org/publications/educational-leadership/feb15/vol72/num05/How-We-Know-Collaboration-Works.aspx.

Applegate, Anthony J., and Mary DeKonty Applegate. 2010. "A Study of Thoughtful Literacy and the Motivation to Read." *The Reading Teacher*, 64(4): 226–234. Newark, DE: International Reading Association.

Armstrong, Thomas. 2003. *The Multiple Intelligences of Reading and Writing: Making Words Come Alive.* Alexandria, VA: Association for Supervision and Curriculum Development.

Baker, Al. 2012. "Despite Obesity Concerns, Gym Classes Are Cut." *The New York Times.* Accessed on January 24, 2014 http://www.nytimes.com/2012/07/11/education/even-as-schools-battle-obesity-physical-education-is-sidelined.html.

Barnes, Bob. 2008. *5-Minute Bible Workouts for Men.* North Eugene, OR: Harvest House Publishers.

Barras, Jonetta Rose. 2001. "Loose Lips." *Washington City Paper.* Accessed on November 19, 2014 http://www.snopes.com/language/document/dcps.asp.

Beck, Hall, Sherry Rorrer-Woody, and Linda G. Pierce. 1991. "The Relations of Learning and Grade Orientations to Academic Performance." *Teaching of Psychology* 18: 35–37.

Beers, Kylene. 2003. *When Kids Can't Read, What Teachers Can Do: A Guide for Teachers 6–12.* Portsmouth, NH: Heinemann.

Borges, Jorge Luis. 1960. *El Hacedor.* Madrid, Spain: Alianza.

Boyer, Ernest L. 1991. *Ready to Learn: A Mandate for the Nation.* Princeton, NJ: The Carnegie Foundation for the Advancement of Teaching.

Brassell, Danny. 2014. *Read, Lead and Succeed: 50 Ways to Produce Extraordinary Results in Business and Life.* Los Angeles, CA: Success Press.

Breheny Wallace, Jennifer. 2014. "Should Children be Held Back for Kindergarten?" *Wall Street Journal Online.* Accessed December 10, 2015 http://www.wsj.com/articles/should-children-be-held-back-for-kindergarten-1410536168.

Brozo, William G. 2010. *To Be A Boy, To Be a Reader: Engaging Teen and Preteen Boys in Active Literacy.* 2nd ed. Newark, DE: International Reading Association.

Bryant, Bear. 2012. "Top 50 Quotes from Bear Bryant." Accessed on September 6, 2015 https://www.saturdaydownsouth.com.

Bryk, Anthony S., Penny Bender Sebring, Elaine Allensworth, Stuart Luppescu, and John Q. Easton. 2010. *Organizing Schools for Improvement: Lessons from Chicago.* Chicago, IL: University of Chicago Press.

Burns, Martha D. 2012. "The Reading Brain: How Your Brain Helps You Read, and Why It Matters." *The Science of Learning Blog* http://www.scilearn.com/blog/the-reading-brain.

Catapano, Susan, Jane Fleming, and Martille Elias. 2009. "Building an Effective Classroom Library." *Journal of Language and Literacy Education* 5(1): 59–73.

Cervetti, Gina N., and Elfrieda Hiebert. 2015. "The Sixth Pillar of Reading Instruction." *The Reading Teacher* 68(7): 548–551.

Chapman, Sandra. 2014. "The Power of Conversation." *Independent School* 73(4).

Chenworth, Karin. 2015. "How Do We Get There from Here?" *Educational Leadership* 72(5): 16–20.

Cherry, Kendra. "Differences Between Extrinsic and Intrinsic Motivation." Accessed October 16, 2014 http://psychology.about.com/od/motivation/f/difference-between-extrinsic-and-intrinsic-motivation.htm.

Churchill, Neil C. and Virginia L. Lewis. 1983. "The Five Stages of Small Business Growth." *Harvard Business Review* 7(1).

Cialdini, Robert. 2009. *Influence: Science and Practice*. Boston, MA: Pearson Education.

City, Elizabeth A. 2014. "Talking to Learn." *Educational Leadership* 72(3): 10–16.

Clark, Christina, and Lucy Hawkins. 2010. *Young People's Reading: The Importance of the Home Environment and Family Support*. London, England: National Literacy Trust.

Clarke, Philip A. C. 1998. "Body Language." Accessed September 28, 2015 http://www.philipclarke.org/sermons/BODY%20LANGUAGE.pdf.

Comcast. 2015. "Internet Essentials." Accessed July 17, 2015 https://www.internetessentials.com/.

Conzemius, Anne E., and Jan O'Neill. 2013. *The Handbook for SMART School Teams: Revitalizing Best Practices for Collaboration*. Bloomington, IN: Solution Tree.

Cullinan, Bernice E. 2000. "Independent Reading and School Achievement." *School Library Media Research* (3): 1–24.

Cuthell, Tom. 2004. "Ebony and Ivory: A Story of Hope." Parish Church of St Cuthbert. Accessed December 1, 2015 http://www.st-cuthberts.net/crgnl01.php.

Davey, Beth. 1983. "Think-Aloud: Modeling the Cognitive Processes of Reading Comprehension." *Journal of Reading* 27(1): 44–47.

DeName, Kristi A. 2013. "Repetition Compulsion: Why Do We Repeat the Past?" *Psych Central*. Accessed June 30, 2014 http://psychcentral.com/blog/archives/2013/06/29/repetition-compulsion-why-do-we-repeat-the-past/.

Disney, Walt. 2015. "Walt Disney Quotes." Just Disney. Accessed July 15, 2015 http://www.justdisney.com/walt_disney/quotes/.

Duckworth, Angela Lee. 2013. "The Key to Success: Grit." *TED Talks Education*. Accessed July 17, 2015 http://www.ted.com/talks/angela_lee_duckworth_the_key_to_success_grit?language=en.

Duffy, Gerald. 2003. *Explaining Reading: A Resource for Teaching Concepts, Skills and Strategies*. New York, NY: Guilford Press.

Dweck, Carol. 2007. *Mindset: The New Psychology of Success*. New York, NY: Random House.

Ericsson, K. Anders. 1996. *The Road to Excellence: The Acquisition of Expert Performance in the Arts & Science, Sports & Games*. Mahwah, NJ: Lawrence Erlbaum Associates.

Ericsson.com. 2015. *Ericsson Mobility Report*. Accessed June 20, 2015 http://www.ericsson.com/res/docs/2015/ericsson-mobility-report-june-2015.pdf.

Federal Communications Commission. 2015. "Lifeline Program for Low-Income Consumers." Accessed November 14, 2015 https://www.fcc.gov/lifeline.

Fisher, Douglas, and Nancy Frey. 2012. "Motivating Boys to Read: Inquiry, Modeling, and Choice Matter." *Journal of Adolescent & Adult Literacy* 55(7): 587–596.

Fisher, Douglas, Nancy Frey, and Ian Pumpian. 2012. *How to Create a Culture of Achievement in Your School and Classroom*. Alexandria, VA: ASCD.

Ford, Henry. 2015. "Henry Ford Quotes." Brainy Quote. Accessed December 1, 2015 http://www.brainyquote.com/quotes/quotes/h/henryford145978.html.

Freedman, Jonathan, and Scott Fraser. 1966. "Compliance Without Pressure: The Foot-in-the-Door Technique." *Personality and Social Psychology* 4: 195–202.

Gagne, Marylene, and Edward L. Deci. 2005. "Self-Determination Theory and Work Motivation." *Journal of Organizational Behavior* 26(4) 331–362.

Gardner, Howard. 1991. *The Unschooled Mind: How Children Think and How Schools Should Teach*. New York, NY: Basic Books.

———. 2011. *Frames of Mind: The Theory of Multiple Intelligences*. 3rd ed. New York, NY: Basic Books.

Garner, David M., and Susan C. Wooley. 1991. "Confronting the Failure of Behavioral and Dietary Treatments for Obesity." *Clinical Psychological Review,* 11: 729-780.

Gladwell, Malcolm. 2011. *Outliers*. New York, NY: Back Bay Books.

Godin, Seth. 2003. *Purple Cow: Transform Your Business by Being Remarkable.* New York, NY: Portfolio Hardcover.

Goleman, Daniel. 2005. *Emotional Intelligence: Why it Can Matter More than IQ.* 10th ed. New York, NY: Bantam Books.

Grolnick, Wendy, and Richard M. Ryan. 1987. "Autonomy in Children's Learning: An Experimental and Individual Difference Investigation." *Journal of Personality and Social Psychology* 52: 890–98.

Gurian, Michael, and Kathy Stevens. 2004. "With Boys and Girls in Mind," *Educational Leadership* 62(3): 21–26.

——. 2014. "The Wonder of Boys." *The MOON Magazine.* Accessed November 18, 2014 http://moonmagazine.org/michael-gurian-wonder-boys-2014-05-02/3/.

Guthrie, John. 2001. "Contexts for Engagement and Motivation in Reading." *Reading Online* 4(8).

Guthrie, John, and Alan Wigfield. 2000. "Engagement and Motivation in Reading." In *Handbook of Reading Research*, edited by Michael Kamil, Peter Mosenthal, David Pearson, and Rebecca Barr, 518–533. Mahwah, NJ: Erlbaum.

Hansel, Tim. 2012. "The Sound of One Hand Clapping." *Chicken Soup for the Unsinkable Soul: Inspirational Stories of Overcoming Life's Challenges.* Pikesville, MD: Backlist.

Hardie, Eric. 2015. "When Students Drive Improvement." *Educational Leadership* 72(9): 92–96.

Harter, Susan. 1978. "Pleasure Derived from Challenge and the Effects of Receiving Grades on Children's Difficulty Level Choices." *Child Development* 49: 788–99.

Harter, Susan, and Guzman, M. E. 1986. "The Effect of Perceived Cognitive Competence and Anxiety on Children's Problem-Solving Performance, Difficulty Level Choices, and Preference for Challenge." Unpublished manuscript. Denver, CO: University of Denver.

Harvey, Stephanie, and Anne Goudvis. 2000. *Strategies That Work: Teaching Comprehension to Enhance Understanding.* Portland, ME: Stenhouse.

Hawkins, Margaret J. 2004. "Researching English Language and Literacy Development in Schools." *Educational Researcher* 33(3): 14–25.

HDCYT. 2007. "Charlie Bit My Finger." *YouTube.com.* Accessed December 1, 2015 https://www.youtube.com/watch?v=_OBlgSz8sSM.

Hempenstall, Kerry. 2006. "What Brain Research Can Tell Us About Reading Instruction." *Learning Difficulties Australia Bulletin* 38(1), 15–16.

Henderson, Anne T., Judy Carson, Patti Avallone, and Melissa Whipple. 2011. "Making the Most of School-Family Compacts." *Educational Leadership* 68(8): 48–53.

Henderson, Anne T., and Karen L. Mapp. 2002. *A New Wave of Evidence: The Impact of School, Family, and Community Connections on Student Achievement.* Austin, TX: Southwest Educational Development Lab.

Hsiao, Aron. 2015. "How did eBay Start? A Brief History of eBay." *eBay.* Accessed December 10, 2015 http://ebay.about.com/od/ebaylifestyle/a/el_history.htm.

Hudson, Alida K., and Joan A. Williams. 2015. "Reading Every Single Day: A Journey to Authentic Reading." *The Reading Teacher* 68(7): 530–538.

International Association for the Evaluation of Educational Achievement (IEA). 2011. *PIRLS 2011 International Results in Reading.* Boston, MA: Boston College School of Education. Accessed July 2, 2015 http://timss.bc.edu/pirls/2011/international-results-pirls.html.

International Society for Technology in Education (ISTE). 2007. *ISTE Standards for Students.* Accessed September 7, 2015 http://www.iste.org/standards/iste-standards/standards-for-students.

Jackson, Jesse. 2015. "Jesse Jackson Quotes." Brainy Quote. Accessed December 1, 2015 http://www.brainyquote.com/quotes/quotes/j/jessejacks161813.html.

Jarrett, Olga J. 2013. "A Research-Based Case for Recess." *U.S. Play Coalition,* 1-6.

Jones, Charley. 2015. "Motivational Speakers Hall of Fame: Charley Jones Quotes." Accessed November 25, 2015 http://getmotivation.com/charlie-tremendous-jones-hof.html.

Jung, Carl. 1939. *The Integration of the Personality.* New York, NY: Farrar & Rinehart.

Kage, Masaharu. 1991. "The Effects of Evaluation on Intrinsic Motivation." Paper presented at the meeting of the Japan Association of Educational Psychology, Joetsu, Japan.

Kanold, Timothy. 2011. *The Five Disciplines of PLC Leaders.* Bloomington, IN: Solution Tree.

Knowles, John. 2003. *A Separate Peace.* New York, NY: Scribner.

Kohn, Alfie. 1993. *Punished by Rewards.* Boston, MA: Houghton Mifflin.

———. 1999. "From Degrading to De-grading." *High School Magazine* http://www.alfiekohn.org/teaching/fdtd-g.htm.

Krashen, Stephen. 2004. *The Power of Reading: Insights from the Research.* 2nd ed. Santa Barbara, CA: Libraries Unlimited.

———. 2005. "Optimist International." *Optimist International.* Accessed November 17, 2014 http://www.optimist.org/default.cfm.

———. 2011. "Protecting Students Against the Effects of Poverty: Libraries." *New England Reading Association Journal 46* (2): 17–21.

———. 2012 "Stephen Krashen Interview–Poverty's Impact on Literacy." By Mike McQueen, *ProfessionalDevelopmentForTeachers.com,* Accessed November 2, 2014 http://www.ProfessionalDevelopmentForTeachers.com/stephen-krashen-interview-povertys-impact-on-literacy.

———. 2013. "Access to Books and Time to Read versus the Common Core State Standards and Tests." *English Journal,* 21. Accessed November 17, 2014 http://www.sdkrashen.com/content/articles/access_to_books_and_times_to_read_versus_the_common_core.pdf.

Kriete, Roxanne, and Carol Davis. 2014. *The Morning Meeting Handbook.* 3rd ed. Amherst, MA: Center for Responsive Schools.

Layne, Steven L. 2009. *Igniting a Passion for Reading.* Portland, ME: Stenhouse Publishers.

L'Engle, Madeleine. 2015. "Madeleine L'Engle Quotes." Goodreads. Accessed September 10, 2015 http://www.goodreads.com/author/quotes/106Madeleine_L_Engle.

Lepper, Mark R., David Greene, and Richard E. Nisbett. 1973. "Undermining Children's Intrinsic Interest with Extrinsic Reward: A Test of the 'Overjustification' Hypothesis." *Journal of Personality and Social Psychology* 28(1):129–137.

Lindsay, Jim. 2010. "Children's Access to Print Material and Education-Related Outcomes: Findings from a Meta-Analytic Review." Accessed August 30, 2014 http://rif.org/documents/us/RIFandLearningPointMeta-FullReport.pdf.

Lundin, Stephen C., Harry Paul, and John Christensen. 2000. *Fish! A Remarkable Way to Boost Morale and Improve Results.* New York, NY: Hyperion.

Madden, Mary, Amanda Lenhart, Maeve Duggan, Sandra Cortesi, and Urs Gasser. 2013. "Teens and Technology 2013." Pew Research Center: Internet, Science & Tech. Accessed November 17, 2014 http://www.pewinternet.org/2013/03/13/main-findings-5/.

Marinak, Barbara, and Linda Gambrell. 2008. "Intrinsic Motivation and Rewards: What Sustains Young Children's Engagement With Text?" *Literacy Research and Instruction* 47(1): 9–26.

Mayo Clinic Staff. 2013. *Stress Relief from Laughter? It's No Joke.* Mayo Clinic. Accessed November 4, 2014 http://www.mayoclinic.org/healthy-lifestyle/stress-management/in-depth/stress-relief/art-20044456.

McQueen, Mike. 2014. *Getting Boys to Read: Quick Tips for Parents and Teachers.* Arvada, CO: Twenty First Century Publishing.

——. 2015. "Leadership for Implementing a Reading Makeover." *Professional Development for Teachers.* Accessed September 30, 2015 http://www.professionaldevelopmentforteachers.com/new-esl-student-part3/.

Medina, John. 2008. *Brain Rules*: *12 Principles for Surviving and Thriving at Work, Home, and School.* Seattle, WA: Pear Press.

Milian, Mark. 2011. "Why Apple Is More Than Just Steve Jobs." *CNN.com Digital Biz.* Accessed September 6, 2015 http://www.cnn.com/2011/TECH/innovation/08/24/steve.jobs.team/.

Miller, Donalyn. 2010. *The Book Whisperer: Awakening the Inner Reader in Every Child.* San Francisco, CA: Jossey-Bass.

——. 2010. "How to Accelerate a Reader." *Education Week.* Accessed November 17, 2014 http://blogs.edweek.org/teachers/book_whisperer/2010/09/reading_rewarded_part_ii.htm.

Miller, Greg. 2010. "How Reading Rewires the Brain." *Science.* Accessed November 14, 2014 http://news.sciencemag.org/brain-behavior/2010/11/how-reading-rewires-brain.

Miller, Rebecca. 2014. "Bold on Literacy." *Library Journal* 139(4) 4–12.

Milton, Ohmer, Howard R. Pollio, and James A. Eison. 1986. *Making Sense of College Grades.* San Francisco, CA: Jossey-Bass.

Mohr, Kathleen A. J. 2006. "Children's Choices for Recreational Reading: A Three-part Investigation of Selection Preferences, Rationales, and Processes." *Journal of Literacy Research and Instruction* 38(1): 81-104.

National Center for Education Statistics. 2013. *The Nation's Report Card: Trends in Academic Progress 2012.* Washington, DC: National Center for Education Statistics, Institute of Education Sciences, U.S. Department of Education. Accessed July 31, 2015 http://nces.ed.gov/nationsreportcard/pubs/main2012/2013456.aspx.

National Governors Association (NGA) Center for Best Practices and Council of Chief State School Officers (CCSSO). 2010. "Common Core State Standards for English Language Arts." Washington, DC: National Governors Association Center for Best Practices, Council of Chief State School Officers. www.corestandards.org.

Neuman, Susan B., and Donna Celano. 2001. "Access to Print in Low-Income and Middle-Income Communities: An Ecological Study of Four Neighborhoods." *Reading Research Quarterly 36*(1): 8–26.

Newhouse, Ronald. 1998. "Friday, May 29, 1998." *Daily Devotions*. Accessed December 10, 2015 http://www.devotions.net/devotions/files/1998/may29.htm.

Nicholson-Nelson, Kristen. 1998. *Developing Students' Multiple Intelligences*. New York, NY: Scholastic Professional Books.

Novotney, Amy. 2013. "Music as Medicine." *Monitor on Psychology* 44(10): 46.

Ohanian, Susan. 2008. "Where Have All the Children Gone?" *Susanohanian.org.* Accessed July 12, 2015 http://www.susanohanian.org/show_commentary.php?id=285.

Peters, Tom. 2005. "Re-Imagine! Business Excellence in a Disruptive Age." World Business Forum, Radio City Music Hall. Accessed April 17, 2015 *tompeters.com/_slides/2005/WrldBiz-NY_091305.ppt.*

Pink, Daniel. 2009. "The Puzzle of Motivation." Accessed September 12, 2014 http://www.ted.com/talks/dan_pink_on_motivation.

Plitnick, B., MG Figueiro, B. Wood, and MS Rhea. 2010. "The Effects of Red and Blue Light on Alertness and Mood at Night." *Lighting Research and Technology* 42(4): 449–458.

Prensky, Marc. 2001. "Digital Natives, Digital Immigrants." *On the Horizon* 9(5): 1–6.

Provine, Robert. 2000. "The Science of Laughter." *Psychology Today.* Accessed June 30, 2015 https://www.psychologytoday.com/articles/200011/the-science-laughter.

Ravi Mehta, Rui Zhu. 2009. "Blue or Red? Exploring the Effect of Color on Cognitive Task Performances." *Science* 27(323):1226–1229.

Raymond, Chris. 2014. "The Exponential Mind." *Success,* 66.

Sastry, Narayan, and Anne R. Pebley. 2008. "Family and Neighborhood Sources of Socioeconomic Inequality in Children's Achievement." Ann Arbor, MI: University of Michigan Institute for Social Research.

Sax, Leonard. 2006. *Why Gender Matters: What Parents and Teachers Need to Know About the Emerging Science of Sex Differences.* New York, NY: Harmony.

Schank, Roger C., and Robert P. Abelson. 1995. *Knowledge and Memory: The Real Story*, edited by Robert S. Wyer Jr. Mahwah, NJ: Erlbaum.

Schein, Edgar H. 1956. "The Chinese Indoctrination Program for Prisoners of War: A Study of Attempted Brainwashing." *Psychiatry* 19(2): 149–172.

Shanahan, Timothy. 2012/2013. "The Common Core Ate My Baby and Other Urban Legends," *Educational Leadership* 70(4): 10–16.

Sinek, Simon. 2009. *Start with Why: How Great Leaders Inspire Everyone to Take Action.* New York, NY: Portfolio.

Smith, Frank. 1988. *Joining the Literacy Club.* Portsmouth, NH: Heinemann.

Smith, Hallie. 2014. "Inside the Brain of a Struggling Reader (Infographic)." *Scientific Learning.* Accessed July 15, 2015 http://www.scilearn.com/blog/insider-the-brain-of-a-struggling-reader-infographic.

Sousa, David A. and Carol Ann Tomlinson. 2010. *Differentiation and the Brain: How Neuroscience Supports the Learner-Friendly Classroom.* Bloomington, IN: Solution Tree.

Stanovich, Keith E. 1986. "Matthew Effects in Reading: Some Consequences of Individual Differences in the Acquisition of Literacy." *Reading Research Quarterly* 21: 360–407.

Stone, W. Clement. 2015. "W. Clement Stone Quotes." Brainy Quote. Accessed September 3, 2015 http://www.brainyquote.com/quotes/authors/w/w_clement_stone.html.

Tomlinson, Carol Ann, and Edwin Lou Javius. 2012. "Teach for Excellence," *Educational Leadership* 69(5): 28–33.

Tough, Paul. 2013. *How Children Succeed: Grit, Curiosity, and the Hidden Power of Character.* New York, NY: Mariner Books.

Tovani, Cris. 2015. "Let's Switch Questioning Around," *Educational Leadership* 73(1): 30–35.

Trelease, James. 2011. The Read Aloud Handbook. 7th ed. New York, NY: Penguin.

——. 2012 "Jim Trelease Interview–Reading Aloud with Struggling Readers." By Mike McQueen, *ProfessionalDevelopmentForTeachers.com.* Accessed November 14, 2014 http://www.ProfessionalDevelopmentForTeachers.com/jim-trelease-interview-reading-aloud-with-struggling-readers.

Tschannen-Moran, Megan, and Bob Tschannen. 2014. "What To Do When Your School's In a Bad Mood." *Educational Leadership* 71(5): 36-41.

Twain, Mark. 1876. *The Adventures of Huckleberry Finn*. Mineola, NY: Dover Publications.

U.S. Department of Education. 2014. "Data Snapshot (School Discipline)." *Civil Rights Data Collection*. Accessed January 18, 2016 http://www.ocrdata.ed.gov/Downloads/CRDC-School-Discipline-Snapshot.pdf.

———. 2008. "A Nation Accountable: Twenty-Five Years After A Nation at Risk." Accessed July 13, 2015 http://www.ed.gov/rschstat/research/pubs/accountable/.

Usher, Alexandra, and Nancy Rober. 2012. "What Nontraditional Approaches Can Motivate Unenthusiastic Students?" *What Can Schools Do to Motivate Students?* Washington, DC: Center on Education Policy. Accessed July 13, 2015 http://www.cep-dc.org/publications/index.cfm?selectedYear=2012.

Van Vechten, Diana. 2013. "Impact of Home Literacy Environments on Students From Low Socioeconomic Status Backgrounds." *St. John Fisher College*. Rancho Palos Verdes, CA: Fisher Digital Publications. Accessed on July 15, 2015 http://fisherpub.sjfc.edu/education_ETD_masters/2013.

Vu, Pauline. 2008. "Do State Tests Make the Grade?" *Stateline*. Accessed September 29, 2015 http://www.pewtrusts.org/en/search#q=Do%20state%20tests%20make%20the%20grade%3F/s=Relevance/pg=0.

Warlick, David. F. 2009. *Redefining Literacy 2.0*. Columbus, OH: Linworth Publishing.

Warner, Claire. 2013. *Talk for Reading*. Leicester, England: United Kingdom Literacy Association.

Wilhelm, Jeffrey D. 2001. *Improving Comprehension with Think-Aloud Strategies*. New York, NY: Scholastic Inc.

Wooden, John. 2015. "John Wooden Leadership Case Study." Leadership With You. Accessed September 5, 2015 http://www.leadership-with-you.com/john-wooden-leadership.html.

Zamosky, Lisa. 2011. "Why Boys and Girls Learn Differently." *WebMD*. Accessed November 26, 2014 http://www.webmd.com/parenting/features/how-boys-and-girls-learn-differently.

Zgonc, Yvette. 2008. "Romancing the Brain." Presentation, SDE Second–Third Grade Teachers Conference, Orlando, FL. November 18–19.

Zimmerman, Frederick J., Jill Gilkerson, Jeffrey A. Richards, Dimitri A. Christakis, Dongzin Xu, Sharmistha Gray, and Umit Yapanel. 2009. "Teaching by Listening: The Importance of Adult-Child Conversations to Language Development." *Pediatrics* 124(1): 342–349.

Resources

Alcott, Louisa May. 1983. *Little Women*. New York, NY: Bantam Dell.

Butler Seder, Rufus. 2007. *Gallop! A Scanimation Picture Book*. New York, NY: Workman Publishing Company.

Caldwell Rinehart, Susie. 2004. *Eliza and the Dragonfly*. Nevada City, CA: Dawn Publications.

Cassidy, John and Brendan Boyle. 2010. *Klutz Book of Ridiculous Inventions*. New York, NY: Scholastic.

Danneberg, Julie. 2000. *First Day Jitters*. Watertown, MA: Charlesbridge Publishing.

Fleischman, Paul. 2004. *Joyful Noise: Poems for Two Voices*. New York, NY: Harper Trophy Publishing.

Griffiths, Andy. 2003. *Just Annoying*. New York, NY: Scholastic.

Griffiths, Andy. 2002. *Just Disgusting*. New York, NY: Scholastic.

Griffiths, Andy. 2003. *The Day My Butt Went Psycho*. New York, NY: Scholastic.

Griffiths, Andy. 2014. *The Very Bad Book*. Sydney, Australia: Pan Macmillan.

Hobbs, Will. 2007. *Crossing the Wire*. New York, NY: HarperCollins.

Hobbs, Will. 1998. *Ghost Canoe*. New York, NY: Avon Books Inc.

Hobbs, Will. 2008. *Go Big or Go Home*. New York, NY: HarperCollins.

Lowry, Lois. 1993. *The Giver*. Boston, MA: Houghton Mifflin.

Jenkins, Steve. 2011. *Actual Size*. Boston, MA: HMH Books for Young Readers.

Martin, Bill and Eric Carle. 1996. *Brown Bear, Brown Bear, What Do You See?* New York, NY: Henry Holt and Company.

Montgomery, L.M. 1994. *Anne of Green Gables*. New York, NY: Dover Publications.

Neuschwander, Cindy and Wayne Geehan. 1997. *Sir Cumference and the First Round Table*. Watertown, MA: Charlesbridge Publishing.

Numeroff, Laura Joffe, and Felicia Bond. 1985. *If You Give a Mouse a Cookie.* New York, NY: Harper and Row.

Oxenbury, Helen and Michael Rosen. 1997. *We're Going on a Bear Hunt.* New York, NY: Little Simon Publishing.

Publications International. 2007. *The Backyardigans Musical Adventure.* Lincolnwood, IL: Publications International.

Reed-Jones, Carol. 1995. *The Tree in the Ancient Forest.* Nevada City, CA: Dawn Publications.

Sabuda, Robert and Matthew Reinhart. 2005. *Encyclopedia Prehistorica.* Somerville, MA: Candlewick Press.

Stillinger, Doug. 2004. *Klutz Book of Paper Airplanes.* New York, NY: Scholastic.

Tang, Greg. 2004. *The Grapes of Math.* New York, NY: Scholastic.

The Editors of Sports Illustrated Kids. 2009. *Wow! The Pop-up Book of Sports.* Boston, MA: Little Brown and Co.

Twain, Mark. 1994. *The Adventures of Huckleberry Finn.* Mineola, NY: Dover Poublications.

Viorst, Judith. 1987. *Alexander and the Terrible, Horrible, No Good, Very Bad Day.* New York, NY: Aladdin Paperbacks.

Notes

Notes

Notes

Notes